FIRE AND ASHES

MICHAEL IGNATIEFF

FIRE AND ASHES

SUCCESS AND FAILURE IN POLITICS

Harvard University Press

CAMBRIDGE, MASSACHUSETTS

LONDON, ENGLAND

2013

Published in Canada by Random House Canada

Text design by Andrew Roberts

First Harvard University Press edition, 2013

Library of Congress Cataloging-in-Publication Data

Ignatieff, Michael.

Fire and ashes : success and failure in politics / Michael Ignatieff.

pages   cm

Includes bibliographical references and index.

ISBN 978-0-674-72599-7 (cloth : alk. paper)

 1. Ignatieff, Michael.   2. Politicians—Canada—Biography.   3. Liberal Party of Canada—Biography.   4. Political culture—Canada.   5. Canada—Politics and government—1993-   I. Title.

F1034.3.I48A3 2013

328.71′092—dc23   2013021522

For Zsuzsanna,
and in memory of
Brad Davis,
Michael Griesdorf
and
Mario Laguë

CONTENTS

ix   *Acknowledgements*

I   ONE: Hubris

7   TWO: Ambition

33   THREE: Fortuna

51   FOUR: Reading the Room

69   FIVE: Money and Language

89   SIX: Responsibility and Representation

115   SEVEN: Standing

137   EIGHT: Enemies and Adversaries

165   NINE: What the Taxi Driver Said

177   TEN: The Calling

185   *Notes*

193   *Index*

ACKNOWLEDGEMENTS

You can't go anywhere in politics without a team who give their all for you. I got as far as I did thanks to a team who started as strangers and ended up as friends. If I've forgotten any of you, please forgive me.

Alfred Apps, Dan Brock and Ian Davey brought me into politics. Senator David Smith and his irrepressible assistant, Jen Hartley, helped mobilize caucus support for my leadership campaign. Former prime ministers Paul Martin and Jean Chrétien gave me advice, some of which I should have heeded. Bill Graham led the party well throughout 2006. Marc Lalonde and Donald S. Macdonald, ministers in Pierre Trudeau's governments, offered me the benefit of their experience, as did Robert and Elinor Caplan and David and Penny Collenette. Adrian McDonald, Carolina Gallo and Nancy Coldham seemed to be at every venue, as were David Wright and Larry Herman. Sachin Aggarwal, Alexis Levine, Mark Sakamoto and Leslie Church formed the core of the team of lawyers and students who ran my leadership campaign; Milton Chan was one of the data monkeys and Tom Allison was an *eminence grise*. Beth Hirshfeld ran my canvassing team. Paula Viola tramped the streets with me before going off to law school. Marc Chalifoux was my personal assistant in 2006. Besides raising money, Elvio and Marlene DelZotto took me under their wing. Abe Schwartz marshalled the video team for the 2006 convention and became a good friend. Mary Kancer was my indefatigable constituency assistant in Etobicoke–Lakeshore; Armand Conant was my official agent; and Jamie Maloney was the president of my riding association. I can still hear his mother, Marion Maloney, fiercely urging me to get more women into my campaign. Kathy Kotris, Annetta Jewell, Natasha Bronfman, Jill Fairbrother, Marti Rowse and Connie Micaleff were the backbone of the Etobicoke–Lakeshore team. I shared the riding with Laurel Broten, member of Provincial Parliament. Jeff Kehoe flew me around southern Ontario through thunderstorms and late-night landings in tiny airstrips. Paul Zed's exuberant driving terrified me on the roads of New Brunswick. Steve Megannety was the "sign guy" who said to me: "Give me my party back"; Kevin Chan gave up a promising career in the Privy Council Office to write policy for me; Adam Goldenberg wrote speeches that I foolishly tried to improve. Peter Donolo served as my chief of staff and with Pat Sorbara, Heather Chiasson and Jean Marc Fournier led the team that ran my office from 2009 onward; Patrick Parisot brought his political and diplomatic experience to bear in the leader's office; Sarah Welch kept us running smoothly; Jeremy Broadhurst brought phlegmatic charm to the management of Commons business; Brian Bohunicky and Michael McNair helped me draft the platform for the 2011 election; Casey Antolak, Dan Langer, Dave Ritchie and Jim Pimblett kept me on the road; Gavin Menzies kept telling me, "You're living the dream." Marc Gendron, Gosia Radaczynska and Jordan Owens led our social media team. Richard Maksymetz, our western organizer, never did give up smoking; Matt Stickney never forgot to have a good time; and Mike O'Shaugnessy mastered duck-walking backward through a crowd.

Trevor Harrison, Christian Provenzano and Rheal Lewis staffed me as deputy leader and together we lived the crisis over the Chalk River nuclear facility in December 2007.

Josh Drache, Expie Casteura and Gerry Petit welcomed us home to Stornoway and made it a refuge for two and a half years. Jane Kennedy looked after Zsuzsanna and me with a tender heart. Scott McCord always knew how to find a way to get us where we had to go.

Ian McKay, executive director of the party, kept the show on the road through a difficult period.

Kevin Vickers, Sergeant at Arms, reminded me, whenever I forgot, that the House of Commons is a place of dignity; Speaker Peter Milliken defended the privileges of Parliament with courage. The director of the party's legislative operations in the House of Commons, Richard Wackid, loved the House too and lost a brave battle to Lou Gehrig's disease.

The members of Parliament and senators who served with me on the Liberal benches between 2006 and 2011 gave me a lesson in politics every Wednesday at caucus and every time we worked together in their constituencies across the country. I also want to thank all of the candidates who stood under my leadership in the 2011 election.

Olivier Duchesneau, Brigitte Legault, Robert Asselin, Paul Ryan, Marc-André Blanchard, Raymond Garneau, Jean-Marc Fournier and Lucienne Robillard did their best to make me understand the politics of Quebec, as Dwight Duncan, Don Guy and Aileen Carroll did in Ontario. No visit to London, Ontario, was possible without Mary Mclaughlin. Dalton McGuinty, premier of the province of Ontario, told me: "There are only two questions worth asking in politics: are you ready to win, and are you prepared to lose?" Premier Jean Charest of Quebec told me the essential word in politics is "*la pérseverance*, Monsieur Ignatieff, *la pérseverance*." In Newfoundland, Paul Antle organized the team and let me rest on his downstairs couch; in Nova Scotia, Jim and Sharon Davis gave us an inspiring example of courage: Jim's son Paul died in service in Afghanistan. In Saskatchewan, the Richardson and Merchant families were unfailing in their support. In Alberta, Grant Mitchell, Joan Bourassa and Daryl Fridhandler kept the flame alive; in British Columbia, Keith and Mary Jane Mitchell were always available to commiserate and Gordon and Kilby Gibson and their daughters were there to advise and inspire. David and Brenda McLean were both generous and welcoming. Jatinder and Rosie Rai were great guides to all the communities of BC's lower Mainland.

Michael Chong of the Conservatives, Peter Stoffer of the NDP and Gilles Duceppe of the Bloc Québécois proved that civility across the aisle was possible in the House of Commons.

André Pratte of *La Presse*, Susan Delacourt of the *Toronto Star*, John Ibbitson and Michael Valpy of the *Globe and Mail* and Craig Oliver of CTV showed that journalists can keep confidences and not betray you. Michael Levine tried to warn me of the dangers I was running, but I didn't listen.

Chris Bredt and Jamie Cameron showed up on the night of defeat, when everyone else had left, and kept us company. Kirsten Walgren and Rob Riemen gave us a break in Amsterdam when we needed it most, and Bernard Haitink and Simon Rattle provided sublime inspiration.

Bob Rae, my friend and rival through five years of political life, served loyally under my leadership and served the party well as interim leader.

Rob Prichard, John Fraser, David Naylor and Janice Gross Stein helped me find gainful employment afterward. David Ellwood, Iris Bohnet, Arthur Applbaum and many other colleagues welcomed me back to the Kennedy School.

The dean of the Law School at the University of Pennsylvania invited me to give the J. Roberts Memorial Lecture in 2012, "Standing in Law and Politics." Brendan O'Leary gave me helpful comments about the lecture. Peter Florence invited me to give the Raymond Williams Lecture on Politics and Literature at the Hay Festival in 2012. The Humanities

Center at Stanford University invited me to give the Presidential Lecture in 2012, entitled "Enemies and Adversaries: Partisanship in Politics," and the Center for the Study of Rationality at the Hebrew University of Jerusalem invited me to give the Edna Ullmann-Margalit Lecture in 2013, "Rationality in Politics." My Kennedy School students in DPI 205— Responsibility and Representation—helped me to understand what this book is trying to say. I want to thank Linacre College, Oxford, for the honour of asking me to give a Tanner Lecture on Representation and Responsibility in June 2013.

Derek Johns of AP Watt saw the point of this book when others did not. Ian Malcolm of Harvard University Press and Paul Taunton of Random House Canada shared Derek's faith, and their editing made it better.

My brother, Andrew Ignatieff, had his doubts about whether this political journey was advisable, but once I was launched on my way, he supported me through every twist and turn.

The book commemorates three men: Brad Davis, a young lawyer who worked on my campaign in 2006 and who died of cancer; Michael Griesdorf, who campaigned door to door with me in 2006 and died in 2008; and Mario Laguë, director of communications in my office, who died in an accident in August 2010. I mourn them all.

Fire and Ashes is dedicated to the one who was there at the beginning, did every mile of the journey and is still there now: my wife, Zsuzsanna Zsohar.

ONE
HUBRIS

ONE NIGHT IN OCTOBER 2004, three men we had never met before—and whom we later called "the men in black"—arrived in Cambridge, Massachusetts, to take my wife, Zsuzsanna Zsohar, and me out to dinner. We met at the Charles Hotel, next door to the Kennedy School of Government, where I taught human rights and international politics. Alfred Apps, a Toronto lawyer, seemed to be the leader. He was voluble; ash flew from his cigarette, wine drained from his glass and he dominated the conversation. Dan Brock was the urbane one, a debonair English-speaking Montrealer with a big Toronto law firm. The third was Ian Davey, a writer and filmmaker with deep-set eyes beneath heavy brows. He was the son of "the Rainmaker," Senator Keith Davey, manager of many fabled national campaign victories for the Liberal Party. After a drink or two, Apps came to the point: Would I consider returning to Canada and running for the Liberal Party?

The Liberal Party was in power in Ottawa then, and I asked if the prime minister, Paul Martin, had sent them. They exchanged glances. Not exactly. The men in black, it seemed, were acting on their own initiative. They were proposing a run from outside, and their ambition, they said plainly, was to make me prime minister one day. Dan Brock said the party was "heading for a train wreck." Without a new leader it would lose the next election. They would put together a team.

Young people would flock to our banner. They would find me a seat and help me win it at the next election, due sometime in the next two years. Would I at least consider it?

It was an astonishing proposition. I had never thought of myself as anything but Canadian, but I hadn't lived in the country for more than thirty years. I'd been a fellow at King's College, Cambridge, a freelance writer in Britain, and now a professor at Harvard. True, I had worked on Prime Minister Pierre Trudeau's campaign in 1968 and I had observed politicians all my life, but why did anyone think my political writing qualified me to become a politician? I was an intellectual, someone who lives for ideas, for the innocent and not-so-innocent pleasures of talk and argument. I'd always admired the intellectuals who had made the transition into politics—Mario Vargas Llosa in Peru, Václav Havel in the Czech Republic, Carlos Fuentes in Mexico— but I knew that many of them had failed, and in any event, I wasn't exactly in their league.[1]

What the men in black were proposing was incredible. I had no idea whether they could deliver any of what they promised. When the meal ended and they headed back to Toronto, I said merely that I would think about it.

Zsuzsanna and I walked silently home along the banks of the Charles River in the autumn darkness. We were happy together. I had astonishing students as well as illustrious colleagues, and we both felt at ease, if not at home, in the States. So what was it now—delayed patriotism? raw ambition? some long-suppressed longing for significance?—that seemed to be knocking me off my moorings? What didn't well up inside me was laughter. It should have. The idea was preposterous. Who did I think I was?

Fire and Ashes is the story of why—soon after, and against the better judgment of some good friends—I said yes to the men in black. It is the story of a brutal initiation, followed by a climb to the summit of politics in the largest democracy by physical size in the world. I want to explain how it becomes possible for an otherwise sensible person to turn his life upside down for the sake of a dream, or to put it less charitably, why a person like me succumbed, so helplessly, to hubris.

This is more of an analytical memoir than an exercise in autobiography. I want to use my own story to extract the wheat from the chaff, to reach for what is generic about politics as a vocation, as a way of life. I lived that life to the full, and for all its dark moments I miss it still. I knew what it was like to speak to four thousand people in a teeming hall, to hold them briefly, or so I thought, in the palm of my hand. I also knew what it was like to speak to a hostile crowd when waves of stony suspicion radiated from every face. I felt the surge of loyalty from the thousands of people who joined our cause and I experienced the sting of betrayal from a conspiratorial few. There were times when I felt I was shaping and moulding events, other times when I watched helplessly as events slipped out of my control; I knew moments of exaltation when I thought I might be able to do great things for the people, and now I live with the regret that I will never be able to do anything at all. In short, I lived the life. I paid for what I learned. I pursued the flame of power and saw hope dwindle to ashes.

Ash is a humble residue but it has its uses. My mother and father used to spade ash from their grate onto the roses against the west-facing wall of our house. My parents are long since gone, but when their roses bloom every summer I like to think it is because I still spade the ashes from the cold fire onto their roots.

The ashes of my experience, I hope, will be dug into somebody's garden. I hope that what I learned from five years in the arena will speak to those who were once kids like me, giving little speeches to themselves as they walked to school, who dreamed of political glory and in adulthood acted out their childhood dreams. Anyone who loves politics—as I still do—wants to encourage others to live for their dreams but also to enter the fray better prepared than I was. I want them to know—to feel—what it is like to succeed, but also to know what it is like to fail, so they will learn not to be afraid of either.

This book is in praise of politics and politicians. I came away from my experience with renewed respect for politicians as a breed and with reinvigorated faith in the good sense of citizens. If this sounds strange, or even disingenuous, coming from someone whose political career ended in failure, I would reply that failure has its privileges. I've earned the right to praise a life that did not go so well for me.

There is so much wrong with democratic politics today—and I will say what I think is wrong—that it is easy to forget what is right about the democratic ideal: the faith, constantly tested, that ordinary men and women can rightly choose those who govern in their name, and that those they choose can govern with justice and compassion. The challenge of writing about democratic politics is to be unsparing about its reality without abandoning faith in its ideals. I lived by that faith, and this book is a testament to the faith that abides with me still.

TWO
AMBITION

THE FIRST THING YOU NEED TO KNOW when you enter politics is why you're doing it. You'd be surprised at how many people go into politics without being able to offer anyone a convincing reason why. But *why* is the first question they—voters, press and rivals—will ask you, and your success or failure turns on how you answer. The truth might be that you want to lead your country because the job comes with a plane, a house, a bureaucracy at your beck and call, and a security detail of men and women in suits with guns and earpieces. The truth may be that you long for power and enjoy the thrill of holding people's futures in your hands. It might be that you are in search of posterity. You want to be famous, to be in the history books, to have schools named after you and your portrait hung in hallowed halls. It might be that you want to settle scores with your past. You want to revenge yourself on everyone who ever said you wouldn't amount to anything.

You wouldn't want to say any of this. There are few rewards for candour in politics. What you say—always—is that you want to make a difference. You believe your experience qualifies you to serve. These circumlocutions are the etiquette of democracy, the ritual salute to the sovereignty of the people. The people themselves may suspect that the difference you want to make is to your own life, not to theirs. But they want to hear you say that you are in it for them.

It's worth considering that such dissembling may have its uses. The pretense may begin as a piece of hypocrisy and end up becoming a politician's second nature. From pretending to serve, you may surprise yourself by actually doing so. Indeed, you have to acquire some sense of service if you are to survive at all. A politician's job can be so thankless at times that if you don't acquire a sense of vocation you turn yourself, by stages, without realizing it, into a hack.

When I began considering the offer from the "men in black," I had to decide, first of all, why I wanted to be prime minister. Let there be no mistake: that was the proposition on offer. I would return home, win election as a member of Parliament, and when the time came, make my bid for power. But why did I want power in the first place? I had almost no sense of political vocation, and I certainly didn't have a good answer to the question of why I wanted to hold high office. What drew me most was the chance to stop being a spectator. I'd been in the stands all my life, watching the game. Now, I thought, it was time to step into the arena. But this is the kind of thing you say to yourself, not to those you're trying to win over. I was to learn this soon enough. In the summer of 2006, when I was campaigning for the leadership of my party, I appeared before the Montreal business community in the white dining room of Power Corporation. One of the business leaders asked me whether I could explain, in just a sentence or two, why I wanted to be prime minister. The question caught me by surprise. I said it was the hardest job any country has on offer. I wanted to see whether I could handle the challenge.

Nothing gets you into more trouble in politics than blurting out the truth. I can still remember the chill my answer spread over that crowd. These were business people who, being leaders themselves, weren't interested in bankrolling my existential challenges. They were looking to support someone who would win and give them access to power.

I learned then that I had the wrong answer to the basic question of what my political life was supposed to be for. Later on, when the climb to the top ceased to be an adventure and became a struggle to survive, I learned just how important it was to have convincing answers to the question of why you were doing it all. Believe me when I tell you that this language of existential challenge is strictly for dilettantes—something I was accused of being.

I can remember a period between September and December 2009, when I was the leader of my party and made mistake after mistake, when the press was brutal and my own staff was so shell-shocked by the plummeting poll numbers that they couldn't look me in the eye. Before the daily ordeal of Question Period (QP), down in the Commons Chamber, when I had to face a cocksure government that had me on the ropes, I would go into the washroom, look at myself in the mirror and force myself to want the job, force myself to believe I could do it, and not just throw in the towel then and there. During this period, Zsuzsanna would say to me: you don't want this enough. But that wasn't the problem. I no longer remembered why I had ever wanted it at all. These are the moments—and they occur in every tough job—when you're no longer sure you're up to it. Your every mistake seems to confirm that you aren't. Your self-confidence is shot. All you know for certain is that you once wanted this and that you have to find that primal desire within if you hope to survive. So it had better be there.

Politics tests your capacity for self-knowledge more than any profession I know. What I learned is this: the question about why you want to be a politician is a question about whom you want it *for*. In my case, whom *did* I want it for?

At the primal level where ambition takes root in a person, you want the things you want in life for the people who made you who you are.

In my case, I wanted political success for the sake of my mother, Alison, and my father, George, because I believed they would have wanted it for me. This is a piece of projection, of course, since they were long dead by the time my political career began. I felt their influence not in any injunctions they ever uttered about the way I should live my life, but rather in the distinguished way they had lived theirs. My ambitions felt less like my own creation than a tradition inherited from them. The Ignatieffs were minor nobility in nineteenth-century Russia who rose to some prominence through service to the czar. My great-grandfather was Russian ambassador to the Ottoman court in Constantinople and later, in 1882, minister of the interior, responsible for restoring order after the assassination of Czar Alexander II. His political career ended in failure, and he spent the last twenty years of his life on his estate in Ukraine, brooding about how intriguers at court had cost him the ear of the czar and how all his plans for Russia had ended in defeat. His son, my grandfather Paul, began his career running the family estates in Ukraine and then rose through the imperial bureaucracy to become deputy minister of agriculture and finally, in 1915, minister of education in the last government of Czar Nicholas II. The Russian Revolution swept him into exile, first in England and then in Canada. He and my grandmother, Natalie, ended their days in a small cottage in Upper Melbourne, Quebec, and are buried in the Presbyterian cemetery overlooking the St. Francis River.[1]

My father, George, was the youngest of their five sons, and the most ambitious. He was sixteen when the family, down on their luck, landed in Montreal from England. That first summer, he went out to British Columbia to work on a railway party laying track in the Kootenay Valley. He learned to drink, swear and cut timber and returned home at the end of the summer of 1928, brown, muscular and a Canadian. He enrolled at the University of Toronto, did well enough to win a Rhodes

Scholarship to Balliol College in Oxford and was there in 1939 when war was declared. He left Oxford and in early 1940 went down to London to serve with the Canadian government at Canada House in Trafalgar Square. There, at the age of twenty-seven, he found himself in a city under German bombardment, working as the personal assistant of Vincent Massey, the heir to the Massey-Harris-Ferguson farm machinery business, then serving as Canadian High Commissioner to Britain. For four years of the war, my father drafted Massey's letters and telegrams and arranged his schedule, sometimes accompanying him to Whitehall for meetings with ministers and generals. Between the British defeat at Dunkirk, in 1940, and 1942, when American soldiers began to arrive in Britain, the Canadian Army was a vital component of the defence of the British Isles. Canada mattered. It was a dangerous but also a glorious time to begin your career as a diplomat for Canada. My father did his professional apprenticeship in the service of an extraordinary man, punctilious and pompous, more English than the English, and yet, for all that, a leader.

My father's working colleagues at Canada House also included Lester B. Pearson, a charismatic diplomat who much later became prime minister of Canada. Many long nights in 1940 and 1941, he and my father took their turn fire-watching together on the roof of Canada House, phoning the civil defence whenever they saw an incendiary catching fire on the roofs around Trafalgar Square. There were raids so severe that they forced the two of them off the roof and into basement shelters, where they huddled in the darkness, feeling the water from ruptured pipes slowly seeping around their shoes. One Sunday morning, after a particularly intense raid, they watched from the roof as charred files from bombed government offices in Whitehall drifted through the air. Pearson said something to the effect, my father remembered, "that civilization could not stand much more of this kind of destruction and that we would have to try to stop it."[2] In my father's mind, at least, Pearson's passionate post-war support for the United Nations flowed from that moment.

There too at Canada House in the middle of the war, my father met my mother, Alison Grant. She was a niece of Vincent Massey: Massey's wife, Alice Parkin, was her aunt. My mother had come to London in 1938, aged twenty-two, to attend the Royal College of Art and was working in MI5, British military intelligence, as a typist and secretary.

My mother's people were just as ambitious and public-spirited as the Ignatieffs. George Parkin, my great-grandfather, was a New Brunswick schoolteacher who managed, by sheer force of personality and cultivation of the powerful, to make himself the founding secretary of the Rhodes Trust, the organization that administers the Rhodes Scholarships in Oxford. Another great-grandfather, George Monro Grant, had been expedition secretary to the railway survey party, led by the engineer Sandford Fleming, that went west in the summer of 1872 to reconnoiter the Yellowhead route through the Rockies to the Pacific.[3] From the high summer heat of July to the early snows of October they travelled by canoe, train, steamer, horseback and Red River cart from the Atlantic to the Pacific. They were the first Canadians to take the measure of the land that had been brought together as a country five years before. When my great-grandfather came home from the journey, he wrote *Ocean to Ocean*, one of the first narratives of the grandeur of the land and its future prospects. If you grew up, as I did, with *Ocean to Ocean* on the bookshelves, you felt you belonged to a family that had been nation-builders.

The Grant side of the family had their stories about prime ministers too. John A. Macdonald—the Conservative chieftain who held the country together with bribery, threats and raw political skill till his death in 1891—was the member of Parliament for Kingston, where my great-grandfather presided as principal of Queen's University. My great-grandfather, known around Kingston as Geordie Grant, had serious moral qualms about Macdonald's methods—extorting cash for his party, for example, from the railroad builders—and he did not hesitate to make his scruples known. The two men met near the end of their lives at a function in Kingston, where Sir John A. approached my great-grandfather and in a joshing manner asked him, "Geordie, why were you never a friend of mine?" "I've been your friend, Sir John," my great-grandfather tartly replied, "when you were right." "I have no use for friends like that!"[4] the old lion replied.

These stories are what kept me to the sticking place when times were difficult. Politics was the big arena, the place where you lived a life of significance, where you measured up to the family imperatives. It was in the blood. I wanted it for them and so I wanted it for me.

Let me confess right now that all this is still the wrong answer to the question of why you should go into politics. You can't lead a political life to live up to your parents. It's also a political error. Any sense of entitlement that you might take from your past is absolutely fatal in politics. The best thing about democracy is—or should be—that you have to earn everything, one vote at a time. I knew enough not to feel entitled. I knew I had to earn it. But the fact that I come from a family with a calling for public life played powerfully in my mind as I considered whether to accept the offer from the men who had come to dinner that October night.

While my mother worked in MI5 she roomed at 54A Walton Street in South Kensington with a tart, diminutive Winnipeg native named Kay Moore, later Gimpel. Between late 1942 and early 1943, they gave a home and a bed to Frank Pickersgill and John Macalister, two Canadians who had joined SOE, the Special Operations Executive, in order to parachute into France and join up with Resistance units combatting the German occupation forces. My mother grew close to Frank—how close I'll never know—in the few months before June 1943, when he left one night to parachute into the dark to a landing spot in the Loire Valley south of Paris. Almost as soon as the pair of Canadians landed, they were betrayed and handed over to the Gestapo, who sent them to a concentration camp. For two years, my mother and Kay waited for word. Special Operations Executive asked them to concoct personal messages that only Frank and John would understand—such as "the samovar is boiling at 54A"—to see if they would reply on their wireless telegraph, but the replies that came back didn't seem to be coming from them. The Germans in fact were playing radio games to mislead the SOE into believing the men were still functioning as agents. Both women began to fear the worst, but it was only in the spring of 1945, when Buchenwald was liberated, that Kay and Alison learned that the two Canadians had been executed there, after torture, months before, in September 1944.[5]

In April 1945, my mother wrote a letter to Frank's brother Jack, in which I hear—as sons rarely do—the authentic sound of my mother's young hopes and dreams:

> I do know that [Frank] was happy in England—his time was very full, and consequently to those of us who were drawn into that circle of unbounded affection, love, and happiness, which he created, the loss cannot be counted.
>
> He bound the household together with his humour, his embracing interest and love of mankind. He set a standard we try to follow. I also know that nothing would have stopped him going—nothing anyone could say or do. He knew clearly and definitely to the day of his departure—he must go. His death is not only a personal loss to a few like myself who know his place will never

be filled. His brand of courage—his courage coupled with his imagination—are not only needed in war, but needed so badly when the war is over, needed by everyone.

But his life wasn't wasted. I feel, as so many of his friends have here said to me, he left us his spirit and faith and uncompromising belief in what was right. That is the legacy he left us. He showed us a way of life and I for one won't forget it ever.

In the fall of 1945, my mother came home from the war and married my father. While she almost never talked about Frank, he was a presence in our home throughout my growing up. It happened that during the 1950s, our house in suburban Ottawa was just a block away from Frank's brother, Jack, and his family. Frank was theirs more than ours, but our house cherished the memory too.

After the war, my mother and father rose through the ranks of the Canadian Foreign Service, and my brother and I grew up in postings overseas: Washington, Belgrade, London, Paris, Geneva and back home in Ottawa. My father worked for several prime ministers, but one of them, Lester Pearson, was always just Mike to him. When I was a child in Ottawa in the 1950s, I once watched Mr. Pearson play baseball at the picnic for the Department of External Affairs, where my father worked and where Mr. Pearson was the minister. It was at a school baseball diamond in the suburbs and Mr. Pearson was at bat, in shirtsleeves and a tie. He bunted and beat out the throw to first base and turned around, foot on the bag, rewarding his employees, all loyally cheering, with a beaming smile.

After the Arab-Israeli war of 1956, my father worked on the team that developed the peacekeeping force for Suez, an effort that won Pearson the Nobel Peace Prize in 1957. In the Arab-Israeli War a decade later, Pearson was prime minister and my father held Canada's seat on the United Nations Security Council. He was one of the drafters of Resolution 242, which remains, to this day, a basis for peace between Israel and the Palestinians.

My father was a pallbearer at Pearson's funeral in January 1973 and bore him to his resting place in Wakefield, Quebec. Just before I entered politics, I went up and paid my respects at his grave. Pearson is buried beside two public servants and close friends—Norman Robertson and Hume Wrong. Pearson, Robertson and Wrong were the epitome of a great age in Canadian government and public service. They wore sober suits and bow ties, crackled with an intimidating intelligence and wore their staffs down with a ferocious work ethic; they were internationally minded, honest as the day was long, small-c conservative in matters financial, liberal in their politics and, in a quiet Canadian way, fiercely patriotic. Theirs was the world I believed in, the example I grew up wanting to emulate. As I said, you want the things you want in life for the people who made you who you are. It never occurred to me, when I returned home and entered politics, that their liberal world and the Canada they had made had long since vanished.

The men my father idealized were people who took for granted that government could do great things. After the 1956 uprising against Communist rule in Budapest, my father helped Jack Pickersgill, then minister of immigration, to get thousands of Hungarians out of refugee camps and settled into a new life in Canada. It was a dramatic gesture by a confident country and my father was proud that he had helped so many people to freedom. The same expansive ambition was at work everywhere in the politics of the 1950s and early 1960s. It was the era when liberal governments in Europe and North America rebuilt their societies and laid the foundation for thirty years of prosperity. In the United States, Eisenhower launched the interstate highway system and the national space program, while Democratic governors in California built the California public university system, a model for higher education the world over. In Canada, a Liberal government built national highway systems and the St. Lawrence Seaway, and found the money to establish new university campuses and national research institutes like the Chalk River nuclear facility, which made Canada a world leader in the production of medical isotopes. The idea was that imaginative government could bind a country together. As soon as I was old enough to join the conversation around the family dinner table, I shared in the idea—or the illusion—that good government—run by people like my dad—was the ultimate solution to any national problem.

My father loved government but he steered clear of party politics, and the stories he told laid bare the difference between the instincts of politicians and of civil servants like himself. He told me about taking notes at a meeting in 1944 between Prime Minister Mackenzie King and a deputation of women—Daughters of the Empire—who were concerned about the impact of pornography (Betty Grable pin-ups and stronger stuff) on the morale of Canadian troops, then fighting their way through Holland into Germany. About a dozen women took their places in King's office and each proceeded to tell him about the terrible effects of pornography. King listened patiently, then stood and went to each and shook their hands gravely, repeating that he had rarely been privileged to have such an important meeting. When the women had been ushered out and silence descended in the prime minister's office, my father cleared his throat and asked Mr. King what actions he wished to authorize. "Get back to work," the PM growled, and waved him out. My father marvelled at King's mastery of dissimulation. It seemed to be the essence of the political life, but my father wanted no part of it.

When I eventually became leader of the Opposition in 2009, it turned out that the office I occupied, the wood-panelled one on the third floor corner of the Parliament Buildings, was the one that had been used by Prime Minister King during World War II. When I sat in the big chair, I would think of my father sixty-five years earlier, hunched over in the corner seat, taking notes on a pad on his knees. The long, panelled room next door to that office was where King's war cabinet had met. Over the door of the cabinet room were two inscriptions: "Fear God" and "Honour the King." Whenever I entered that room, I felt the institutional history calling on us to rise to the occasion.

When I was eighteen, I won an extemporary public-speaking contest for the province of Ontario, and a Toronto newspaper, the *Globe and Mail*, interviewed me and took a picture of me holding the trophy. The reporter asked me what I wanted to do with my life and I said, without pausing for thought, "I want to be prime minister."

Looking back now, I see myself as a child, perhaps an orphan, of the sixties, formed by a politics that now seems only a distant memory. I was fourteen when John F. Kennedy took the oath of office that shining day in January 1961, and I remember watching as the young president stepped forward to shield the page from the sunlight as the aging poet, Robert Frost, stumbled over the reading of his inaugural poem. Later, my schoolfellows and I imitated Jack Kennedy's Boston accent and took to copying one of his characteristic gestures, the way he held his left hand in his jacket pocket, with the thumb protruding over the seam. I can still remember where I was on the stairwell in Upper Canada College when a friend behind me tapped my shoulder and whispered, "I just heard on the radio. The president has been shot."

I was part of the generation whose dream of politics was shaped by the fallen president. The ardour I felt within, I detected in my friends. When I met Bob Rae, the brightest friend I had at the University of Toronto, I noticed that we had more in common than just the fact that his father, Saul, and mine had been friendly rivals at the same university thirty years before. I noticed that when he stood on a student platform, waiting to speak, he held his left hand in his pocket, with his thumb down the seam.

We both entered the University of Toronto just as the demonstrations and teach-ins against the Vietnam War were sweeping through American campuses and beginning to sweep north into Canadian ones as well. With friends like Jeff Rose and Bob Rae, I threw myself into anti-Vietnam politics, helping to organize a teach-in on the war and later taking part in the sit-ins against the presence on campus of recruiters from Dow, the manufacturer of napalm. I also campaigned for the Liberal Party in the autumn election in 1965, going door to door for a fine MP, Marvin Gelber, who was seeking re-election against a formidable opponent, David Lewis, the leader of the Canadian New Democratic Party, the social democrats to the left of the Liberals. It was my first election, and I loved the atmosphere of campaign rooms and zone houses and canvassing teams. We campaigned hard but our man lost, and so my first experience of Liberal politics was defeat.

In early 1968, as a student at the University of Toronto, I went to St. Lawrence Hall to see Pierre Trudeau, then minister of justice in the Pearson government, launch his campaign for the leadership of the Liberal Party (Mr. Pearson had announced his resignation a short time before). I'd never felt such a wave of attraction for a political leader sweep over me. Here was a law professor, an intellectual fresh from the battle to free his province from the dead hand of the Catholic Church and the reactionary, union-busting government of Maurice Duplessis. I was entranced by Trudeau's charm and elusiveness, but most of all by his authenticity, his evident struggle to remain himself in the cauldron of publicity and politics. I see now that he was often amateurish, pretentious even, as he took his first steps into the ring. He was struggling to control the forces he had unleashed and to remain true to the inward, introspective person that he was. I see now how decisive his influence was upon me when, forty years later, I contemplated my entry into the ring. He had entered politics in his late forties, right out of a university classroom. If he could do it, why couldn't I? It was what I thought, though I was certainly no Trudeau.

Trudeau appealed to me because his message combined an implacable refusal to appease nationalist sentiment in his province with a passionate commitment to bring Quebeckers into the centre of our national life. What made him such an inspiring figure was that he knew exactly why he was doing politics and whom he was doing it for. We were sure he was doing it for our generation.

In April 1968 I was pulling wavering delegates over to his side on the floor of the Ottawa Convention Centre at the National Liberal Convention when the fourth ballot tally came in. I watched him rise from his seat in the stands and wave to the roaring crowd that had just elected him the leader of the Liberal Party of Canada and, by virtue of that fact, the next prime minister of the country.

He called an election almost immediately to seek a mandate, and I travelled with him on his campaign plane as a national youth organizer as he swept toward his first election victory in June 1968. He was the kind of leader who would saunter down the plane, sit down beside a young staffer like me, and start an interrogation about the book I was reading. I still remember that it was by Viennese architect Victor Gruen, about city planning.[6] Trudeau sat beside me in the plane, high above the Prairies, and as I stammered out incoherent answers about the book's ideas, I felt the steely eyes of a prime minister sizing me up. When the plane landed, we would race to the venue, him in the lead car of the motorcade, me way in back with the baggage handlers. I didn't have much to do at the events beyond keeping the crowds at bay. Trudeaumania was at its height and I'd never seen such human frenzy before, the way people grabbed at his hands as he worked a rope-line and the way young women screamed and tried to kiss him. There is a demonic side to the passions that can sweep through a political crowd, and I found it intoxicating to watch.

That summer of 1968 also witnessed the dramatic crest of Eugene McCarthy's and Robert Kennedy's insurgent campaigns against President Johnson and the Vietnam War. In February 1968, McCarthy had challenged Johnson in the New Hampshire primary and, thanks to an army of young people, forced Johnson to withdraw from the presidential campaign. Bliss was in that dawn to be alive, to be twenty-one and to feel that the political activism of your own generation could be that powerful.

Exhilaration and a dawning sense of our power were not the only emotions from that time. There was also despair and terror. Martin Luther King was assassinated in Memphis on April 4, 1968, his last sermon, from the night before, warning, with agonizing prescience, that like Moses he might not see the Promised Land, but his people surely would. The night of King's death, Robert Kennedy made a campaign stop in Indianapolis and broke the news to a black crowd. In the darkness, he sought to calm the raw grief and anger in their hearts. He quieted them in a gentle Boston voice, telling the crowd that he had lost a brother, also to an assassin, and that they must grieve together and learn, as the poet Aeschylus taught, to "bear the awful grace of God."[7] I see now how deeply I was inspired by these transcendent examples of what politics should be. Months later, Trudeau's plane was somewhere over Sudbury, Ontario, on June 4, 1968, when the captain's voice came over the intercom and announced that Robert Kennedy had been assassinated in a hotel kitchen in Los Angeles, the night of his conclusive victory in the Democratic primary in California. I remember the devastation of that moment, the stunned awareness dawning on very young people that the exhilaration of the political life we were living could also bring with it violence and utter loss.

Just three weeks after Kennedy's assassination, Pierre Trudeau appeared on the reviewing stand of the St. Jean Baptiste Day parade in downtown Montreal, several nights before the election. As the leading federalist politician of his time, he was the target for all the nationalist and separatist rage in his native province. Bottles and beer cans from jeering separatist demonstrators rained down around him, and his security detail tried to pull him to safety. Trudeau's courage that night was an electrifying sight. I never forgot the display of raw, intransigent political will caught on camera when he pushed restraining hands away and stood to face the anger of the crowd alone.

A week later, after his election victory, his office phoned and invited me out to Harrington Lake, the prime minister's country residence in the Gatineau hills outside of Ottawa. Jennifer Rae, a strikingly beautiful and seductive staffer on his campaign, was his companion in those days. She was the sister of my college friend Bob Rae, and it may have been Jennie's idea for me to come out to keep them company. Trudeau had just taken possession of the place and neither of them seemed quite at home in the rambling, old-fashioned country cottage with the views onto the lake. We swam off the dock and talked about books, anything rather than politics, and I can remember thinking that he had won the greatest victory of his life and he didn't know what to do with it. It was as if the sheer enormity of what he had achieved—storming to the very top of his country's politics in a mere three years—was suddenly dawning on him. He was withdrawn, remote, trying to call up inner resolve for the demands ahead. I caught a glimpse then of the price of glory, the fear it can engender in even the most fearless of men.

That was the last time I saw him in office. My father continued to work for him as an ambassador and Trudeau occasionally turned to

him for advice on foreign affairs. In 1978, when Trudeau was looking to appoint a governor general—the Canadian head of state and
Queen's representative in Canada—he let it be known that my father
was his first choice. For months my father and mother prepared for
the job, accompanying the Queen on a visit to Canada and learning
royal protocol and etiquette. Vincent Massey, my mother's uncle and
my father's first boss, had been governor general, and my father would
be the first son of immigrants to be selected for the post. It was so
much a foregone conclusion that the appointment leaked to the press.
At the last moment, Trudeau, seeking votes out west, changed his
mind and chose a former premier of Manitoba for the job. Low political manoeuvres don't save sinking ships, and Trudeau's manoeuvre
made no difference. He lost the 1979 election anyway. My father, on
the other hand, was crushed. My brother remembers it as the only
time he ever heard my father cry.

Watching my father recover in the years afterward was perhaps my
earliest education in resilience. He picked himself up, wrung out the
frustrated ambition and went on to the noblest decade of his life, serving as chancellor of the University of Toronto while caring for my
mother, who was then drifting into Alzheimer's disease. My father
told me once that failure had been the best thing to happen to him.

Much later, when Trudeau had left power, we met in London, and
we were even filmed together once in the early 1990s, staging a
rather self-conscious conversation for his memoirs about Antigone
and tragic conflicts in politics.[8] We never spoke about my father, who
by then was dead.

Back then, when I worked for him, the lure—of Trudeau himself—
was so strong that I felt I had to pull myself out of his force field. At
the end of that summer, I left Ottawa and set my course to go to
Harvard for graduate work. I had no skills and wasn't ready to remain

in Ottawa and become a staffer in some minister's office. In any case, the euphoric days when I could be invited out to Harrington Lake were over. Layers of bureaucracy now separated me from the man I admired. I was only twenty-one. It was time to get away and acquire some weight. It took thirty-seven years before I came back to politics with, I hoped, the weight I needed.

These stories of mother and father, of Trudeau and Pearson, the tragic and inspiring echoes of Kennedy, McCarthy and King in the United States, shaped my ambitions and propelled me toward politics. But let's be clear: genetics isn't destiny and a family history isn't fate. My brother, Andrew, three years younger than me, was the heir of the same family history, lived the same period of the sixties and felt no impulsion to run for office. He thought I was crazy to put our good name in jeopardy. I chose the family mythology as much as it chose me. When the three strangers invited me to go into politics, it was as if I had been waiting my whole life for them to show up.

The picture they drew of the political landscape back home was grim indeed. The Liberal government of Paul Martin had just survived being defeated in the election of June 2004 and was heading toward collapse, divided by infighting and tarnished by a financial scandal in Quebec. Martin was a decent, principled man who had fought for twenty years to get to the top and now gave the appearance, rightly or wrongly, of being out of his depth. He had been a tough and imaginative minister of finance, but as prime minister, he was being lampooned as "Mr. Dithers." Like Gordon Brown in Britain, Martin had schemed to hold the crown, and now that it was his, it was turning to dust. The Liberal Party had lost its capacity to recruit good people, had little or no support in the West or British Columbia, and after eleven years in power under Martin's predecessor, Jean Chrétien, it had run out of ideas. I was being asked to board a ship heading for the rocks.

The pitch from my new political friends was that it was time for a new captain. They drew a flattering picture of me: proud Canadian with an international reputation, a history in the party going back to Pearson and Trudeau, rhetorical skills, good French. Being an outsider, I had no dog in the fights tearing the party apart and no connection to the scandal then dragging it down in Quebec. Would I think it over?

Given how it all turned out, I should have asked harder questions. Questions like, how were we supposed to win the next election? How was I supposed to revive a party that had been bleeding votes for a decade? I must have assumed we were "the natural governing party" and someone would have the answers. We were still the most success-ful party of government in the democratic world. What I didn't grasp was that a great franchise had reached the end of the road.

As I weighed up my options, I knew I could never take an active part in American politics. I wasn't a citizen and I couldn't even per-suade myself to get an American Green Card. My colleague and close friend Samantha Power would soon leave the Kennedy School and enlist in the service of a newly elected junior senator from Illinois, Barack Obama, but I knew that if I stayed in the United States, I would only be able to watch from the sidelines. If I wanted to get into the arena, it could only be at home. We had our own republicans—the recently re-formed Conservative Party of Canada, under the leader-ship of Stephen Harper—and it was clear that he was in politics to roll back everything I'd ever believed in: national programs that strength-ened the spine of common citizenship, equal rights for all Canadians, and a balanced foreign policy, staunchly independent and internation-alist. I could be a liberal spectator in someone else's country or I could be a liberal activist in my own. The choice seemed obvious.

I did ask myself how I was supposed to overcome my evident liabil-ities. I'd been back and forth to Canada throughout my life, writing, teaching, making films, giving lectures, but I'd played no part in the battle over the constitution in the 1980s, the near-death experience of a referendum on Quebec separation in 1995. You can't find yourself a place in the politics of a country unless you have lived its dramas, and I could be accused of having been missing in action. Still, all my convictions about politics were Canadian. I saw my country as an example of civility, tolerance and international engagement for people the world over. I must have thought that sheer romantic faith in my place of birth would make up for the fact that I hadn't actually lived there.

I gave a lot of thought to the question of what story I would tell if I came home. Every politician has to have one. Indeed, devising, controlling and imposing your story on the public mind is the central task for anyone seeking public office. In my case, my story had to turn my obvious liability—years out of the country—into a strength. There was only one possibility: I would tell my story as a homecoming. It was one of the oldest ones in the book: the prodigal's return. In the Bible, didn't everyone turn out to embrace him when he showed up on the dusty road?

By this point, you have every reason to be tired of the self-dramatization and self-importance in this search for the motives that led me into politics. All I would say is that self-dramatization is the essence of politics. You have to invent yourself for public consumption, and if you don't take yourself seriously, who else will?

The idea of homecoming was authentic, at least to me. Wherever else I'd been in life, home was still my Aunt Helen's cottage on Wreck Island in Georgian Bay, my Uncle Dima and Aunt Florence's Quebec farm, now owned by the Keenans, my family's three-bedroom house in Toronto and, most of all, the cemetery in Upper Melbourne, Quebec, where they had all come to rest: Count Paul, my grandfather; Countess Natalie, my grandmother; my father; my mother; all my aunts and uncles; and one day, I knew, myself.

From the mid 1990s, long before the men in black came calling—I began spending more time in Canada, teaching in Banff so my children could have a summer horseback riding and rafting in the Rocky Mountains, taking Zsuzsanna across the country by car so she could experience the big-sky country of the Prairies for herself, giving the Massey Lectures on the Canadian Broadcasting Corporation. In these lectures, called "The Rights Revolution," I tried to define Canada's political uniqueness: the fact that we didn't have capital punishment or a right to bear arms; that we believed in group rights to protect the French language and aboriginal title to land; the fact that we believed a woman's right to choose should prevail; the fact that a bilingual national experiment, always under stress, forced us constantly, as a condition of survival, to try to understand each other and reach common ground.[9] Americans could afford red state/blue state partisanship; we couldn't. Compromise was built into our way of doing politics. Or so I thought.

I'd been a happy cosmopolitan all my life, but I'd become aware that the price of expatriation was rising. When you live in other people's countries, you eventually bang up against glass doors and cordoned-off areas reserved for insiders. You realize you understand only what the insiders say, not what they really mean. I felt I was welcome everywhere but belonged nowhere. Besides, expatriation is a form of free-riding on other people's politics, just as cosmopolitanism is the privilege of those with passports from somewhere else. Mine was from Canada. It was time to go home.

It took a year, between October 2004 and December 2005, to engineer my return. During that time, the team that the men in black had promised began to take shape. I didn't choose them. They chose me. I flew back to Toronto and found myself being grilled by tough political professionals who wanted to figure out whether, as they say, I had 'legs.' Young law students—like Sachin Aggarwal and Milton Chan—quizzed me on my position on gay marriage (I was for) before signing on. I had lunches with Liberal grandees such as Senator David Smith and former premier David Peterson, and with Liberal fundraisers like Elvio DelZotto. Thick briefing books on public policy issues—health care, energy, jobs—began to arrive in the mail, prepared by young policy thinkers like Alex Mazer, Sujit Choudhry and Michael Pal. I devoured the briefs and felt a growing excitement at the idea that I might be able to do something about the problems my young researchers were laying in front of me: the income inequality that was shocking for a country that liked to think of itself as egalitarian; the weakening of our manufacturing base; the absence of a national energy strategy for a country that was a globally important producer of energy; the increasing alienation between voters and the political system; and the traditional issues of national unity—the divide between Francophones and Anglophones, and the emerging divide between the big cities and the remote and rural regions of a vast country. I studied all these problems and came away thinking that since I had studied them, I must know something about them. I hadn't yet realized that political knowledge is something quite different: knowing an issue in your guts, not just in your head, and knowing which cause must become your battle cry.

In March of 2005, the Liberal Party held its biannual policy convention in Ottawa, and our team persuaded the party president, Mike Eizenga, to invite me to give the keynote speech to several thousand delegates. I'd never spoken in front of so many people before. I began by telling them: "In the United States, where I work, liberals are in the wilderness. In Canada, liberals are in government. Down there, being a liberal is a burden. Up here, it's a badge of honour."

The serried ranks of delegates stretched out in front of me gave me a round of applause for that, and warmed by their reaction I spelled out what liberalism meant to me. When my mother offered someone a liberal portion of pie, I told the delegates, it was always a generous slice. Liberalism, I said, should never lose its association with generosity: of heart, of spirit, of imagination, of vision. I concluded with this:

> Generosity is more than a welcome to strangers. It is an attitude toward ourselves. It means trusting each other, helping without counting the cost, taking risks together. Generosity means keeping our heart open to others, dreaming together that we could be better than we are. That's how this country has always been. This party's job is to keep it that way. Generosity. Unity. Sovereignty. Justice. And the courage to choose, the will to govern. These are the beacons of a liberal politics.[10]

When the speech ended, I was surrounded by clamouring delegates, hands reaching out to me, cellphone cameras flashing and the press waiting to interview me, among them an old friend, Graham Fraser. He whispered, "Good speech," and then realizing I really was about to take the plunge gave me the commiserating look old friends give you when they know they can't stop you doing something foolish.

The day after the speech the prime minister, Paul Martin, asked to see me. I spent an hour in his office while his assistant, Jim Pimblett— later to become mine too—perched in an alcove like a beady-eyed marmoset, never taking his gaze off me. The prime minister sounded me out about Canadian–American relations, but he was really trying to see what I was made of. He was gracious, but he could not have been pleased with my speech or with its reception. I was too obviously a rival. Later, I was given to understand by his people that they would not help me find a seat to enter Parliament. I would have to fight my way into the party on my own.

After meeting with the prime minister and then with Marc Lalonde, one of Pierre Trudeau's closest advisors, who pronounced himself happy with my political progress, the die was cast. I would leave Harvard at Christmas, take a job at the University of Toronto and make a gradual entry into Canadian politics.

Once the decision had been taken, Zsuzsanna and I had dinner in a restaurant in Toronto's Chinatown with Bob Rae, my college room-mate, his wife, Arlene, and one of their daughters. Bob had been in Canadian politics all his adult life, first as a federal member of Parliament for the New Democratic Party and then, between 1990 and 1995, as the first NDP premier of the province of Ontario. His defeat in 1995 had been brutal, but he had got over it and was making a good living as a lawyer in Toronto. When I told him I was going into politics, he exploded. I hadn't earned the right. He had put in the years and who did I think I was? I was taken aback. He wasn't in our party, so what gave him the right to tell me I couldn't fight for a seat as a Liberal? I didn't say any of this, but I should have had it out with him. In retro-spect, his furious reaction was a crucial moment. I hadn't understood that my old friend's political ambitions were far from over and that he was contemplating a switch to our party. I misjudged him as he misjudged me, and we both assumed, wrongly, that old friendship would enable us to work out our rivalry. After all, Gordon Brown and Tony Blair had met in a London restaurant in the early 1990s and agreed that Blair, not Brown, would contest the Labour leadership. Had Rae and I made such a pact, our political careers might have ended differently, but who's to say that one of us would really have deferred to the other? Frankly, I don't believe competing ambitions can ever be reconciled, even between friends.

The die may have been cast and the decision made, but it did not stop both Zsuzsanna and me from many longing backward glances at the life we were leaving behind. But we felt the undertow of adventure sweeping us on, and late that summer, Zsuzsanna turned to me and said with a smile, "What do we have to lose?"

We had no idea.

THREE
FORTUNA

I'D ASSUMED, IN MY INNOCENCE, that my return to Canada would be a leisurely stroll back home, first teaching at the university and then making my move into politics. Suddenly, events, not my own calculations, took charge. In late November 2005, the Liberal government of Paul Martin lost a vote of confidence in the House of Commons, and the prime minister called a general election for January 23, 2006. If I was going to enter politics, this had to be the moment.

When I taught politics, I loved teaching students Machiavelli's *The Prince*. They found his cynicism thrilling and contemporary, but they had wondered what to make of that chapter about the goddess Fortuna. In chapter 25, composed in 1513, right after Machiavelli had been thrown out of Florentine politics, tortured and sent back to his estates in disgrace, he wrote—from bitter experience—that the goddess Fortuna rules politics. Fortuna is a fickle woman, he infamously said, who must be courted, wooed and won. The language Machiavelli uses is famously offensive to modern ears: "it is better to be headstrong than cautious for Fortune is a lady. It is necessary, if you want to master her, to beat and strike her. And one sees she more often submits to those who act boldly than to those who proceed in a calculating fashion. Moreover, since she is a lady, she smiles on the young, for they are less cautious, more ruthless and overcome her with boldness."[1]

Once you set aside his metaphors, Machiavelli's insight endures. Politics plays itself out beneath the gaze of a fickle goddess. Practical politics is no science, but rather the ceaseless attempt of wily humans to adapt to what Fortuna throws in their paths. Its basic skills can be learned but they cannot be taught. While a painter's medium is paint, a politician's medium is time: he must adapt, ceaselessly, to its sudden, unexpected and brutal changes. An intellectual may be interested in ideas and policies for their own sake, but a politician's interest is exclusively in the question of whether an idea's time has come. When we call politics the art of the possible, we mean the art of knowing what is possible *here and now.* The possible includes the potential. Where an average politician sees only a closed room, a visionary one sees the hidden door at the back that leads to a new opportunity. What we call luck in politics is actually a gift for timing, for knowing when to strike and when to bide your time and wait for a better opportunity. When politicians blame their fate on bad luck, they are actually blaming their timing. Only fools believe they can control it. It is simple prudence to be modest about what you can actually control in a political career. Harold Macmillan, a British prime minister of the early 1960s, was asked what was the most difficult aspect of doing his job. "Events, dear boy, events," the old master is supposed to have replied.[2] A wise politician understands that all you can do is exploit events to your advantage. While politicians are always condemned for opportunism, being a skillful opportunist is the essence of the political art. A poor opportunist in politics is simply someone who looks, all too obviously, like he is *exploiting* an opportunity. A skillful opportunist is someone who persuades the public that he has *created* the opportunity.

The timing of my entry into politics was not of my choosing, but I thought, as one does, that I could turn circumstances to my own advantage. I had taught Machiavelli, but I had not understood him. I thought I could master time, only to discover that it would master me.

Over many months, my Toronto team and I had been courting a distinguished member of Parliament, Jean Augustine, hoping to persuade her to resign, after close to thirteen years on the job, and let me stand for nomination in her place. In late November, she announced she wouldn't run again and lent her support for my candidacy to replace her in Parliament. I taught my last class in Wiener Auditorium at the Kennedy School, posed for a photograph with the students and took a flight to Toronto with Zsuzsanna for what we thought would be a routine nomination as Liberal candidate for the riding of Etobicoke–Lakeshore, a district of about a hundred and twenty-five thousand people in the western suburbs of the city.

The scene of my political initiation was a hotel with a Wagnerian name, the Valhalla Inn, a seventies-style banquet hall and airport hotel just off the highway between downtown Toronto and Pearson International Airport. Now it has been flattened to make way for condos, and when I pass the spot these days I sometimes wonder whether it ever existed.

As the airport limo drew up in front of the Valhalla Inn on that cold December night in 2005, the parking lot, the entrance and the lobby were filled with several hundred demonstrators chanting, "Shame! Shame! Shame!" and holding placards that read "Iggy go home." I'd thought I *was* home. Some of the demonstrators were wearing George Bush masks and were denouncing me for supporting the invasion of Iraq. Others, in bright orange Guantanamo jumpsuits, were there to condemn me as an apologist for torture, on the basis of a drastic misreading of a book of mine called *The Lesser Evil*.[3] Most vociferous of all were a crowd of Ukrainian Canadians who came to abuse me for being a Russian chauvinist on the basis of my father's origins and what again, to put it charitably, was a misreading of a passage in *Blood and Belonging*, written thirteen years earlier. In that book, I had made some ironic remarks about Ukrainian independence conjuring up "images of embroidered peasant shirts, the nasal whine of ethnic instruments, phony Cossacks in cloaks and boots and nasty anti-Semites."[4] Nobody seemed to have read the irony in these words or the later passages that clearly supported a sovereign and independent Ukraine.[5] For the demonstrators crowding around our car, however, what I had said in 1993 was only a pretext. A group of Ukrainians, led by a sitting MP in the Liberal caucus, had wanted to put one of their own in the Etobicoke–Lakeshore seat and they were furious that I had frustrated their designs by making "a deal" with Jean Augustine. So they fastened on something I'd written years before to mount a last-minute battle to deny me the nomination.

This aspect of politics—tendentious political misreading of something you said years before—was new to me. I was fully prepared to take responsibility for what I'd actually written, but what I had written wasn't the issue. It never is. The issue is how your opponents turn your "record" to their advantage. "Oppo research," the search for incriminating clips, photographs or sentences ripped out of context, has become a key tool in the arsenal of modern politics, and the ferrets that specialize in "oppo research" have a vast new hunting ground on the Internet. In the age of Facebook and Twitter, you have to choose between never saying or doing anything that could be used against you or letting the chips fall where they may. I'd vote firmly to let the chips fall. You can't hold your life hostage either to the ingenious malice of your opponents. If you stop saying what you think now, you'll forget what it's supposed to sound like when you finally get the chance.

As we surveyed the demonstrators through the limo windows, I felt a comic desire to explain. I wanted to tell the young men and women in George Bush masks, "If only you had seen what I had seen in northern Iraq in 1992, how Saddam had gassed the Kurds, you would understand why I believed he had to go." To the people in the Guantanamo jumpsuits, I wanted to say, "If you'd actually read *The Lesser Evil*, you would know I despise torture as much as you do."[6] It was all a misunderstanding. I could explain everything. I had yet to grasp that in politics, explanation always comes too late. You never explain, you never complain. If you're lucky, you just get your revenge.

Inside the car, with the demonstrators baying at us on the other side of the smoke-tinted windows, Zsuzsanna and I looked at each other. For a split second, I felt like turning around and heading back to Harvard, but her gaze sent an unequivocal message. This wasn't exactly how we'd imagined the homecoming, but there was only one thing to do: get out and fight.

We pushed our way through the protesters and the television cameras and reporters who had come to see the fun and I fought my way through the lobby to the podium in a sweltering hotel ballroom. My team had assembled a crowd of supporters up front and they were clapping and cheering while the crowd at the back of the hall tried to drown me out. The placards they waved told the story. My nomination was anti-democratic, a stitch-up. I was an enemy of the Ukrainian people. I was an apologist for George Bush.

I remember being full of indignation. How could the Ukrainians accuse me of despising them? My great-grandmother and grandfather were buried in Ukraine.[7] When I visited there, I told the crowd, the people had greeted me with the traditional gifts of bread and salt. If they had welcomed me as a friend, how could my fellow citizens take me as an enemy? And besides, I said, why did we persist in dividing ourselves this way? I wasn't Russian and they weren't Ukrainian. We're just Canadians. I shouted myself hoarse above the chants—"Shame!

Shame! Shame!"—coming from the Ukrainians and the protesters in the Guantanamo jumpsuits, and the "I like Mike!" coming from our own people.

The Valhalla Inn was my first exposure to politics as raw combat. Truth be told, I rather enjoyed myself. I exuded righteous indignation at the bad faith of my accusers. I had yet to learn that good or bad faith doesn't come into it. In politics as combat, any stick will do, and in combat what matters is not proving your good faith but winning. That night I prevailed. The men in black had brought in the national party president, Mike Eizenga, to oversee my nomination, and there were party lawyers there to ensure that it was all done according to the rules. I was duly nominated by the assembled party members, despite the baying crowd, and then spirited out the back door and whisked off for my first meeting with my election team.

They must have been in shock, as I was, at the opposition to my candidacy, but as we shook hands and got to know each other, I knew they were all I had. They were local community people from the riding, less than a dozen in all, including the formidable Marion Maloney, in her wheelchair, and Jamie Maloney, her son, at her side; Armand Conant, a real estate lawyer who was to become the official agent for my campaign; Mary Kancer, Jean Augustine's assistant, and several other veterans of Jean's small organization. Jean called her team "the little engine that could," and as I looked them over the team seemed little indeed, but I was wrong about them. They turned out to be devoted people and they are friends still. They could not have known what they were in for by throwing in their lot with me, but they stuck with me to the very end.

I was now nominated, possibly the most controversial candidate in the Toronto area. Over the next fifty-five days, my campaign team— a mixture of downtown lawyers, computer whiz kids and local community people—tried to turn me into a competent politician. It wasn't easy. I must have been a comic sight when I began canvassing door to door, believing that every voter deserved a Socratic dialogue of many minutes' duration. My team would roll their eyes and drag me away to the next house.

Without realizing it at the time, I had passed through the looking glass into the unique psychic world of anyone seeking public office. I was about to spend the next five years of my life in a state of constant dependence on the opinion of others. A French writer of the nineteenth century, Ernest Renan, once called a nation "a daily plebiscite," and for those seeking public office, democracy is exactly that, a daily plebiscite where you assess, every second of the day, how people look at you in the street, how they greet you when you come up and shake their hand, how they react when you come down the aisle of an airplane and settle into your seat.[8] Nobody who has not run for office can quite understand how dependent you become on this daily plebiscite, on the cues, the smiles of recognition, frowns of disapproval that citizens send you when you are out in the public square. I counted on it more than I counted on the polls. The former mayor of New York, Ed Koch, was reputed to have said, hundreds of times a day as he progressed through New York City, "How'm I doin?"[9] Now I understood that this was indeed the question. How *am* I doing? How do *you* think I am doing? My own answers to this question scarcely mattered. I put my fate in the hands of everyone I met. I had no idea how completely this ongoing, minute-by-minute scrutiny by my fellow citizens would take me over and begin to shape my sense of my own worth.

As I canvassed for votes in the shopping malls, apartment blocks and snowy suburban streets of Etobicoke–Lakeshore, I would search every face for signs of support, learn to evaluate subtle cues of indecision, evasion or outright rejection. People, by and large, are astonishingly polite to canvassing politicians, but they also send you signals. The man who takes your flyer through the window of his car, then rolls it up and drives on, is telling you he's never going to vote for you in a million years. The woman drying her hands on her apron when she comes to the door, but stays to hear your pitch, just might come over; the old man who tries to get you inside to have a good chat is just lonely; the young woman who pops her earphones out of her ears at the subway stop and nods approvingly when you make your pitch about funding higher education is going to vote for you, if she actually remembers to show up on election day. I began to understand who my natural constituency was and who was beyond my reach. We had support among young people, educated professionals and minority groups, but we were losing out to the Conservative Party in the wealthier districts in the riding, among the houses with the big driveways, and we were having to compete hard with the New Democratic Party, to the left of us, to hold unionized workers and poorer households in the south of the riding. We were the party in the middle, and we'd run the country for most of the twentieth century by owning the middle ground, but I could feel our support bleeding away from both sides.

We took over a disused bank at a busy intersection as our headquarters—I had a windowless cupboard to myself in the basement vault—and the place was soon swarming with campaign workers. If you love politics, campaign offices are wonderful places. It is organized chaos: half-drunk cups of coffee everywhere, the remains of Chinese take-away and pizza strewn on tables, Hungarian soup prepared by my wife, perfect strangers streaming in and out, press hanging around waiting for an interview, young pols in back rooms filled with maps, marked in colours to denominate friendly from enemy territory. We even had a minister of the church, Rob Oliphant, who was to become a fine member of Parliament himself, drop by the office regularly to offer spiritual advice, especially to me. The core of the operation were the "data monkeys," young men and women, grey-faced and sleep deprived, staring at the canvassing returns on computers, figuring out, in the murk of battle, where we stood.

In the chaos of that disused bank, I saw, for the first time, what a political party could be. In a time of social fragmentation, where we are ever more walled off by class and income, race, religion and age, where so many people live alone, where the public square feels deserted, a political party is the place where strangers come together to defend what they hold in common and to fight in a common cause. Whenever the canvassers would flood in and be handed their polling sheets, before they went out to knock on doors in the snowy streets, I would stand on a rickety chair in the middle of the room and tell them that they represented not just me or their party. They represented the best of the country. A political campaign like ours broke down the barriers of race, ethnicity and class that keep us separate. I had never worked with such astonishing diversity: the Ahmadiyya Muslims, led by a Pakistani military man, Major Khalifa, who flocked in to leaflet the riding at night; the Italian carpenters who hammered in the lawn signs; the Caribbean communities who had supported my predecessor, Jean Augustine, and now, at first hesitantly, came out to work for me; the students and young lawyers, led by Brad Davis, Milton Chan, Mark Sakamoto and Sachin Aggarwal, drawn into my campaign because of the chance it gave for their generation to renew their party; the magnificently robed Somali women from the Maybelle, a multi-storey housing project in the north of the riding; Polish Catholics who managed to reconcile their faith with our party positions in favour of gay marriage and abortion; some Ukrainians, including the pastor of a local church, Father Terry, who stood against the hostile tide in their own community; and a phone bank of canvassers who made their pitch for our party in a babble of a dozen different languages.

Certain individuals stood out. Steve Meganetty, the "sign guy," a tall, white-haired man in jeans with a deadpan drawl, plastered the whole constituency with our election signs. He was a long-time party veteran who drove an hour and a half each way from his home in Niagara to help me out. He was sick of the party infighting that had broken out when the current prime minister, Paul Martin, had forced out his predecessor, Jean Chrétien, in 2003. Since that time, a once-great national institution had fragmented into warring clans. When I asked Steve why he came down every day to work for me, he said simply, "I want my party back."

Then there was Baljit Sikand, a warm-hearted Sikh man who always sported amazingly stylish and highly coloured turbans and who ran the Bloomingdale Limousine Service, with dozens of drivers, from a small cabin beside a greenhouse in Etobicoke. If you had Baljit on your side, you had a sizeable portion of the local Sikh community, and you also had the benefit of the unparalleled local intelligence that anyone who runs a taxi and limousine service in a community is bound to acquire.

It was a December-January campaign and I did three canvasses a day, dressed in a parka I had once bought for a trip to the Arctic, together with snow boots, snow pants, toque and gloves. The sun went down at 3:30 p.m., so we slogged through the snowy streets in the dark, my canvass team and I, determined to show that the "carpetbagger," the "parachute candidate," as my opponents were calling me, could earn it the hard way.

We knocked on thousands of doors, and I still remember some of the encounters. There was the lady who came to the door, drying her hands on her apron, with a little boy in tow. "Brian here has asthma," she said. "What are you going to do to get the pollution out of the air?"

I did my best, half-frozen in her doorway, to give her an environmental platform she could believe in, but as she went back inside to finish getting Brian his supper, I wondered whether I had made the sale, and I felt the gulf that separates voters' preoccupations from the rhetoric of policy platforms. But I also began to understand, from this encounter and a hundred others, that I was doing politics for her.

A young couple in tears opened the door on Christmas Eve, and when I said I would come back later, they beckoned me in and told me they had just returned from a funeral for their nephew. He had been out with some friends when they had been caught in a sudden exchange of gunfire between two drug gangs. Their nephew, barely twenty years old, had been struck in the back by a stray bullet and killed instantly. I went to the memorial service for him down at City Hall several weeks later. When, in Parliament, we led the fight against the government's attempt to dismantle Canada's gun laws, I was standing up for those grief-stricken constituents I had met on Christmas Eve.

Politics at the doorstep also give you the measure of the divided worlds that it is a politician's job to reach across. I remember an elegant woman in a baronial doorway at the end of a winding driveway, questioning me on the party program and then dismissing me by saying she couldn't possibly vote for any party that would raise her taxes. Then there were the miserable, unlit, stinking apartment buildings where immigrant families would not open their doors, and those poor young adults who did were half-naked, tattooed, eyes wide open with crack and gone to the world.

Our local campaign drew support from Liberals across Toronto, and as we gained in experience, we gained in enthusiasm. The national trend, however, was going the other way. We had gone into the election thinking our party would win. The Liberal government had cut the deficit, and our methods of restoring fiscal discipline in the 1990s, however brutal, were admired worldwide. The economy was growing and the prime minister was widely credited with creating the conditions for sustained prosperity. But we had been in power for thirteen years and both the party and the government were visibly tired. We were also tarnished. In the wake of the 1995 referendum that had almost resulted in a victory for Quebec separatism, the government had authorized a program to sponsor events in Quebec that would boost the image of Canada in the minds of Quebeckers. Some of the money, millions of dollars in fact, had found its way into the wrong hands, and half a dozen crooked operatives had skimmed some into their own pockets. The prime minister had ordered an inquiry and guilty parties had gone to jail, but the Conservatives were baying for our blood over the "sponsorship scandal" and the public seemed to be agreeing with them.

In the middle of the election campaign came a thunderclap. The Royal Canadian Mounted Police, the Mounties, announced an investigation into whether the Liberal minister of finance had leaked market-shifting information to brokers and investors in the stock market. The accusation was absurd and the police eventually acquitted him of all blame, but once the police stepped into the election campaign and announced their investigation, an unprecedented interference in a national election, our lead in the national polls evaporated.

Ten days before election day, the "data monkeys" came to me with long faces, saying we were running behind. The Conservative Party was beginning to surge. So confident had they become that Stephen Harper, the leader of the party, came to the big Ukrainian cathedral in the riding and called on the assembled crowd to "send Ignatieff back to Harvard." We summoned an army of canvassers and I knocked on doors from eleven in the morning until nine thirty at night, while my wife manned the phones at the constituency office and cooked meals to keep us going. On the final weekend of the campaign, the Liberal

Ukrainian faction disgruntled at my candidacy walked into the Conservative headquarters in the riding and switched their support to my opponent, whereupon the New Democratic national leader, Jack Layton, sent out thousands of robo-calls baldly announcing that our campaign was disintegrating and that all progressive voters should come over to them. All in all, it was a wild end to the campaign.

On election night, January 23, 2006, against expectations and thanks largely to the influx of nearly five hundred canvassers, we won handily in Etobicoke–Lakeshore. I had learned the simplest lesson in politics: show them you want it. We showed them, and the people gave me their support. It is a strange, ennobling experience to be given such a vote of confidence and trust from thousands of fellow citizens. Up to that moment, I had spoken only on behalf of myself. I had been responsible only for my family and myself. Now I had to speak for strangers and be responsible to them.

In the packed basement of the Hollywood, a local discotheque and dance bar, with television cables laid across the floors and the lights glaring, I thanked these perfect strangers, my fellow citizens and also the hundreds of volunteers who had made victory possible. Zsuzsanna had copied out a Hungarian poem for me to read if I won, and I liked the sober and simple message it sent. Ian Davey, one of the men in black, whispered, "Lose the poem": I read it anyway, József Attila's final lines of "By the Danube":

> *I want to work. It's hard for human nature*
> *To make a real confession of all that we've done.*
> *The Danube, which caresses the past, present and future,*
> *Has pulled us in, tenderly, as its swift waters run.*
> *From the blood of our fathers shed in former wars*
> *Flows peace, a common memory and mutual regard,*

To put order in our common affairs: this is our task.
And it will be hard.[10]

It was an odd thing to read out in that noisy basement discotheque, packed with waving supporters and journalists, and almost certain to confirm the impression that I was an intellectual landed from outer space, but I didn't mind. "Putting order in our common affairs" became one of the ways I used to define my vocation in politics in the years ahead.

Barely an hour later, still in the basement of the Hollywood, we all watched as the polls closed and the voters across the country gave Stephen Harper and the Conservatives a narrow victory. They had a plurality of seats and votes, but not enough to command a majority in the House of Commons. Just as I was adjusting to this reversal of fortune, and realizing that my political career would actually begin on the opposition benches of Parliament, Prime Minister Martin appeared on television to concede defeat and announce that he was resigning as party leader. A leadership campaign for his successor would begin immediately. The camera crews and journalists who had come to see whether the "parachute candidate" could land safely were now crowding around asking me whether I would be a candidate in the race. If so, the journalists implied, I would be the front-runner. In a blaze of camera lights, Fortuna had taken charge of my life.

I barely remember the weeks that followed, apart from coming up to Parliament for the first time, attending the first meeting of the Liberal caucus and listening while departing and defeated MPs spoke to their caucus colleagues for the last time. We who had survived should have listened more carefully to those defeated colleagues. We thought the Conservative victory was temporary. We, the natural governing party, would be back soon. We kept reassuring ourselves with the idea that we had been sent to "the penalty box." Defeat was merely a time out. That was my first lesson in the encapsulating effect of illusion in politics, how everyone ends up saying the same thing, even though it happens to be wrong. Our defeated colleagues, some in tears as they remembered their time in office, seemed to know better. They were saying, "You may not realize it now, but you are headed off into the wilderness." Little did we know how far ahead the desert sands of opposition stretched out in front of us.

In the weeks before the new Parliament was convened into session and I had to take my seat for the first time, the men in black reappeared and we met to figure out how to run a national campaign for leadership. We had assumed the race would be years ahead, and now it was right in front of us, with a national convention designated for Montreal in December. There would be forty-five hundred delegates, elected in the 308 ridings across the county, and they would choose the next party leader at the Montreal convention in a secret ballot. We did not know it then, of course, but this would prove the last time in our politics that a leader would be actually selected at a delegated convention like this. It promised to be a raucous and hotly contested affair, and we had to get ready. Volunteers were signing up for the fight, and money—we would need millions—was beginning to come in. This was no time for me to play Hamlet. Was I in?

Nothing had turned out as we had expected, but Zsuzsanna and I both understood that we had come back for this and that, despite my lack of political experience, we might never have a better opportunity. So we were in. Truth be told, I felt like a trainee skier starting a descent at the top of a black diamond run. I could hear the ice beneath my skis and I could feel the downward momentum of acceleration. But I told myself I had taken the chair to the top of the hill. Now I had to get myself safely down.

Eight weeks after winning my first election as a member of Parliament, having only just sworn my oath as an MP, I announced my candidacy for the leadership of the Liberal Party of Canada. Ahead of me stretched nine months of a transcontinental leadership race that would take me to every part of the country, and to places inside me I had not known existed.

FOUR
READING
THE ROOM

THE SHEER PHYSICAL CHALLENGE of a national leadership campaign in a country our size began to sink in. We are, after all, the largest democracy by size in the world, a vast country of six time zones, five regions and two official languages. The leader of the party was to be chosen in December in Montreal by delegates nominated by about sixty thousand members in each of the 308 ridings, spread across five thousand kilometres of the country from the Atlantic to the Pacific, from north of the Arctic Circle to the American border. To win the leadership, I would have to win over a majority of these delegates, whether they lived on aboriginal reserves up north, in fishing out-ports down east or in fancy apartment towers on the west coast. Hundreds of thousands of kilometres and thousands of handshakes, parleys, late-night negotiations, deal-making meetings and fundraising rallies lay ahead.

In the weeks that followed my own announcement, twelve candidates entered the race, experienced men and women who had held elective office and served as ministers in government. All of them knew more about politics than I did. It was a strong field and it included Ken Dryden, the former goaltender of the Montreal Canadiens; Stéphane Dion, a Quebecker who had bested separatist nationalists in debate in the 1990s; and last but not least, my childhood friend Bob Rae, who had left the New Democratic Party and joined the Liberals in order to contest the leadership.

I thought I had the edge on Bob, since I had won a seat in Parliament and he had not run in the election. My convention speech the year before had put me in front of thousands of delegates, and the media were giving me a lot of space, intrigued by the story of my homecoming. Senator David Smith worked the caucus with consummate skill, and a lot of seasoned politicians signed on to my candidacy because they thought I could win. These endorsements created a paradox. I was the outsider's outsider and yet here I was, within weeks of entering the race, becoming the Establishment candidate. This created tensions within my own team. The young people who ran my campaign wanted to turn the party upside down. The political professionals who lined up behind me mostly wanted to keep the party the way it was.

The minute you enter a political arena, your opponents begin defining you, and if you don't fight them off, you can lose control of your candidacy. I was now saddled with the label of Establishment candidate and opponents outside the party set about defining me as a George Bush apologist. When I appeared at the University of Ottawa to give a speech early in my leadership campaign, a huge crowd turned out, and right in the middle of my talk, three hooded figures, made up to look like the prisoners at Abu Ghraib, stood up and remained silently standing throughout my speech. I did my liberal best with the situation, telling the crowd that the protesters were welcome, but with the national media watching, it was obvious that the student opposition outside the party was having some success in defining me as an apologist for everything—like torture and abuse of detainees—that I abhorred as much as they did.

As we tried to make sense of these pressures and counter-pressures and the deluge of media coverage, my team and I did grasp that media attention does not win you convention delegates. You earn support one handshake at a time. If you don't show up where the people live, you won't get their vote. In my case, showing up and demonstrating that I could earn support the hard way was especially important if we were to lay to rest the image of the elitist and entitled dilettante.

So we hit the road. For nine months, like all the other candidates in the race, Zsuzsanna and I, together with our assistant Marc Chalifoux, lived on airplanes and in airports. We took the large planes that get you there fast and the small four-seaters, flown by my friend Jeff Kehoe, that get you there slowly at two thousand feet above the lonesome expanse of prairie and forest, the isolated farmhouses with a single porch light on, the vast dark expanses where you look out the window and the sheer immensity of your country begins to dawn on you. We fell asleep in hotels with low-ceilinged, ill-lit corridors and ruined trays of food outside the doors; we lived on Tim Hortons steeped tea, yogurt and biscuits; we kept all hours and found ourselves able to sleep standing up or sitting down, especially in deserted airport lounges late at night. We did so many miles on back roads in the car borrowed from Marc's parents, who ran a dairy farm, that he said we should title our memoirs *The Buick Regal Years*.

Once you enter politics, you are always on show. You never jump a queue, you never get impatient with a driver or a waitress or a check-in clerk. You never lose your temper. You never fail to light up when someone comes over for a picture or an autograph. You surrender the entirety of your private life for the duration. People are watching.

Many successful people, contemplating entry into politics, disdain the endless meet-and-greet, the forced bonhomie of life under the public gaze, as beneath their dignity, but they are wrong. The grind of politics, the endless travel, the meetings, the impossible schedule, the constant being on show are all in search of an authority that can be acquired in no other way. You have to learn the country.

What a good politician comes to know about a country can't be found in a briefing book. What he knows is the way the people shape place and place shapes the people. Few forms of political expertise matter so much as local knowledge: the details of the local political lore, the names of the dignitaries and power-brokers—mayors, high school coaches, police chiefs, major employers—who must always be named from the platform. Great politicians have to be masters of the local. They have to at least remember every place they ever set foot in. Wherever they are, they have to give the impression of being at home. When they ask someone in a crowd where they hail from, they should be able to produce a story that neatly connects them to that voter with the jolt of human recognition. A French expression of praise for a politician is that he is *"un homme de terrain."* There is no exact equivalent in English but there should be. It means he knows the terrain, has his feet planted on the ground, knows where his people come from. I knew many *hommes*—and *femmes*—*du terrain* in politics. I can remember flying with a member of Parliament into his constituency on the east coast and watching him staring intently down at the farms we passed on our approach to the landing strip. "That one is for us," he said, pointing to one house. Then, waving at another one next door, he said with a grimace, "That so-and-so wouldn't vote for you if you got down on your knees and begged." He knew his terrain, house by house, farm by farm, back road by back road, with the unsentimental eye of a farmer appraising a herd.

As long as democracy demands this local knowledge of a politician, as long as it makes this the criterion of credibility and trust, the country should be all right. As soon as democracy loses its connection to place, as soon as the location of politics is no longer the union hall, the living room, the restaurant and the local bar and becomes only the television screen and the website, we'll be in trouble. We'll be entirely in the hands of image-makers and spin doctors and the fantasies they purvey. Politics will be a spectacle dictated from the metropolis, not a reality lived in the small towns and remote communities that are as much part of the country as the big cities. For all the talk about the Internet as the enabler of democracy, the Internet could cause us to lose the aspect of politics that makes it truly democratic: the physical contact between voters and politicians. YouTube videos and ads are no substitute for an encounter between real flesh-and-blood human beings. If the Internet takes over politics, there will be no reality check, no moment left when a voter gets the chance to look at a politician in the flesh and make the decision to trust or not to trust, to believe or not to believe. Politics has to stay corporeal because trust is corporeal.

I think back now to the Knights of Pythias Hall in Springhill, Nova Scotia, the Sam Hughes Legion Hall in Lindsay, Ontario, or the Floata Seafood and Chinese Restauarant in Vancouver's Chinatown. These and countless others were the scuffed-up venues of our country's democracy. On the walls there were the flags and banners, the portraits of the Queen and former prime ministers together with the insignia of the local Lions or Rotary Club. When you walked in, there would be tea and coffee urns together with sandwiches on a table at the back, banquet chairs spread out in a semicircle around a podium and the party faithful ranged in front of you, many retired and semi-retired, the farmers in baseball caps, the union men in T-shirts with their union local on them, the women in sensible dresses and shoes. There was an air of quiet decency about them and a polite skepticism that you were there to overcome. They were the delegates and they had the power.

Four times a day, sometimes more, during that long leadership campaign, I would stride into one of these venues and soon be shaking hands with complete strangers, trying to figure out who they were and what they wanted to hear, giving a short stump speech, taking questions, signing some posters and then moving on to the next airport, the next hall, falling asleep in the next hotel room at the end of a long day.

To get a hearing with them, you had to know what they wanted to hear. The professionals call it "reading the room," and when good politicians read a room right, they will have the audience in the palm of their hand. When they get it wrong, they will die a slow death up there under the lights. I died my fair share of deaths until I learned to unlearn everything I had known up to that point. I had to unlearn being clever, being rhetorical, being fluent, and start appreciating how much depends on making a connection, any connection, with the people listening to you. I learned to find some story from my own life that would tell them, in so many words: I *know* you and you know *me*. In Quebec I would talk about the dairy farm my uncle and aunt (mostly my aunt) ran in Richmond. In the Maritimes I would talk about my great-grandfather from New Glasgow and my grandmother born in Fredericton. These roots, which had been a little abstract to me before, became real to me now. Out west, I talked about my dad's time laying track in the Rockies. I did what all politicians do: I tried to make my story their story.

In appealing to delegates, I was also talking to members of a party that had just been thrown out of office and was struggling to regain its confidence and sense of direction. I told each delegate in every room that I was the candidate of change and renewal. I was untainted by the scandals that had damaged the party brand. But I was also a loyalist, with Liberal roots going back forty years. It was a delicate line to walk. I was running to lead a party whose culture of intrigue disgusted me, but I was seeking votes from loyalists who wouldn't vote for me if my disgust were too plain. I needed to convince them—handshake by handshake, answer by answer, smile by smile—that I had what it took, that I was prepared to work for it and that they could trust me.

Politics is intensely physical: your hands touch, clasp and hold, and your eyes are always reaching for contact. None of this came naturally to me. I had a bad habit of looking down and away when people talked to me. I'd always put my trust in words and let the words do the work, but in politics, the real message is physical, delivered by your eyes and your hands. Whatever you say, your body must communicate the message: you can trust me.

Now that I was in the fray, I admired the masters of the art even more, and I thought back to a master class I had been given in politics in 2001. I was steering Bill Clinton through a room at the Davos meetings at the Waldorf Astoria in New York. I was amazed at his ability to remember names—and not just names but whole family stories—as he squeezed this hand, leaned in to kiss that cheek, locked his gaze on another's, and kept moving, baling them in like a combine harvester. When I met President Obama later on, I will never forget the grip on my elbow, the quick mention of a book of mine, a reference to a mutual friend, Samantha Power, and his casual grace, together with the capacity to make you feel, when you were speaking, that you were the only person of interest to him in the room.

These are ancient arts, the skills that are commended in Baldassare Castiglione's *Book of the Courtier*, written in the early sixteenth century and based on his experience at the court of the Duke of Mantua. The word he used to describe the key talent in politics was *"sprezzatura."* It is also without an exact equivalent in English but basically means the gift of making people feel at ease in your company. Castiglione's advice speaks down the ages:

> I have discovered a universal rule which seems to apply more than any other in all human actions or words: namely, to steer away from affectation at all costs, as if it were a rough and

dangerous reef, and (to use perhaps a novel word for it) to practice in all things a certain nonchalance which conceals all artistry and makes whatever one says or does seem uncontrived or effortless. I am sure that grace springs especially from this ...[1]

"Uncontrived and effortless": the great politicians make contrivance look uncontrived. All of the human skills in politics involve artifice, but the artifice must be concealed with ease and grace. This artificial graciousness can be learned with time and experience, but it cannot be taught. It's not a technique or a routine. There is no executive leadership course that will give it to you. It is a form of gracefulness in human behaviour that is more akin to athletic ability than technical intelligence. If natural grace isn't there to begin with, it can't be acquired or displayed with any conviction. When we call a politician a "natural," we mean she has this mysterious ability to make a connection with others, to make them feel at ease, to make them feel special. All naturals get better with practice, but unless it comes naturally, it doesn't look real. What must be real is not so much the smoothness for which politicians are both envied and despised, but real curiosity and interest in people's stories, in the way they tell them and the meaning they are trying to convey. Of all the qualities that go into *sprezzatura*, I would rate listening, being able to deeply listen to your fellow citizens, as the most underrated skill in politics. For what people want in a politician, what they have a right to demand, is to be listened to. Often, listening is all you can do. Their problems may not admit of a political solution, or at least not a solution you can devise. People will accept that you cannot solve their problems if you give them all of your attention, looking into their eyes, never over their shoulder at the next person in line.

I was learning all of this for the first time, and I was up against some stiff competition, rivals for the leadership who were strong candidates with longer histories in the party than mine, all of them with lots of experience with the arts and skills of politics, all of them with the ability to put a name to a face and call in old favours.

As we travelled the country, I learned that people's inner map of political concerns begins with the local and widens out to the provincial and national. It is an inner map that pays no attention to constitutions and jurisdictions. People would always ask me questions, and if the question was about the local hospital shutting down or a daycare centre closing in their community, you couldn't duck it by telling them that none of it was under federal jurisdiction. People won't listen to you on national issues unless you display literacy about local ones, and the literacy test was tough to pass. We were once in Esterhazy, a small town in rural Saskatchewan that both Zsuzsanna and I had visited before we entered politics. It's a place on the plains where the Hungarian pioneers came in the 1880s to settle the land, and there is a haunting graveyard on a hill outside of town where some of them are buried. My wife, being Hungarian, pronounced the town's name the way she did back home, with a short *a*, but when I did so from the platform, there were frosty looks from the crowd. They all pronounced it with a long *a*. Your ability to connect with people could turn on a detail as small as the right vowel sound.

The intensely local nature of politics often left me wondering what exactly we did share as a people and as a country. It is the politicians' job to speak for what we share, but at first there didn't seem to be much in common at all.

This felt especially true in Quebec. I had thought my French was pretty fluent, but it was tested when I was campaigning for delegates in those rural parts of the province where the majority speak only French and have such a strong accent that it can be hard to understand. Establishing trust in a second language can make you feel as if you're talking long-distance on a bad line. Besides, my French was more Parisian than Québécois, a fact the nationalists in the province kept pointing out. It took me a while to get comfortable and to feel I could command a hearing. My wife said that I changed when I spoke French: I made more expansive gestures and I hammed it up a bit more.

Quebeckers have wanted many things from our national politics, but it all comes down to one big thing: recognition of their distinct identity as a people. It remains an amazing achievement that a French colony of sixty thousand souls defeated by the British in 1759 has grown into a dynamic, close-knit and passionate community of nearly eight million people. But for all their success, they never forget they are an island of French speakers in a continent of three hundred million English and Spanish speakers.

Our party had a visceral connection to Quebec. The party's real founder, Wilfrid Laurier, was the first French-Canadian prime minister, and since Laurier, three Quebeckers—Louis St. Laurent, Pierre Trudeau and Jean Chrétien—have served as party leader and prime minister. Our vocation as a party had always been national unity, drawing French and English together in common cause, but corruption scandals had been draining away our credibility in the province and we were losing seats to the separatist Bloc Québécois on the left and Stephen Harper's Conservatives on the right. Even the New Democrats, long marginal to Quebec politics, were making inroads into the Liberal vote in the province.

Regaining our credibility in Quebec was crucial if we were to return to power. At every stop in Montreal, Quebec City, the little communities on the north shore of the St. Lawrence and the farmland on the south shore near the American border, I reminded delegates that Quebec was the place that took in my Russian family and gave them refuge. I talked about the graveyard overlooking the St. Francis River where they were all buried and how I wanted it always to be part of my country. It had always seemed to me that offering Quebec more powers within Canada was both divisive and beside the point. The real issue was to demonstrate a conviction that the country as a whole was unthinkable unless Quebec and Quebeckers were at the heart of it.

In late June of 2006, when Quebeckers were getting ready to celebrate their holiday, the Fête de la Saint-Jean-Baptiste, a journalist asked whether, given what I had written about nationalism in my book *Blood and Belonging* in the 1990s, I thought Quebec was a nation. It was neither an innocent question nor an academic one. The separatists in Quebec had been insisting that they were a nation, and that as such, they deserved an independent state of their own. Two referenda had been fought on these issues, and the separatists had come within sixty thousand votes of winning the last one in 1995. In *Blood and Belonging*, thirteen years before, I had written: "Because we do not share the same nation, we cannot love the same state."[2] But nations, I went on to say, can *share* the same state and I believed we always would. Of course Quebec was a nation.

No sooner had I finished the interview than I experienced the extraordinary difference between words spoken by a writer and words spoken by a politician seeking national office. That single remark triggered a countrywide debate. Some columnists called me brave, others an idiot savant. All my competitors in the leadership race were forced to declare their own positions, some for, some vehemently against. For a time, Quebeckers, especially young ones, flocked to our banner because we had seemed to recognize them in a way our party had not done before.

In politics calling a fact a fact can be the equivalent of pulling the pin out of a hand grenade. As far as I was concerned, it was a fact that francophone Quebeckers have a national identity: they've always identified both as Quebeckers and as Canadians. It doesn't make their loyalty to Canada less strong, but it makes it more complex. The genius of our politics lay in the fact that we had never imposed a single national identity on anyone. We were not a country founded on *e pluribus unum*—out of many, one—but instead a complex quilt of overlapping identities. We had created a country in which you could be Quebecker and Canadian in whatever order you chose. What I rejected about separatism was not the pride in nationhood but the insistence on a state, the belief that Quebeckers must make an existential choice between Quebec and Canada. This was a choice most Quebeckers had always refused to make, for the very good reason that they felt some loyalty to both. They wanted to be Quebeckers and Canadians in whatever order they believed right. It was a kind of moral tyranny on the part of separatists to force them to choose between parts of their own selves. After much travail, I said, we had understood that countries must be built on freedom of belonging. From this followed our system of federalism. We could not centralize power in this country, I said, because we could not centralize identity.

No sooner had my words been uttered than English Canadians began asking whether I was putting the national unity of the country at risk, while nationalist Quebeckers wanted to know when I would recognize their nationhood in the Canadian constitution. I replied that I was against opening the Pandora's box of our constitution. Our habit of turning every political question between Quebec and Canada into a constitutional negotiation was a serious mistake. Aha, said the Quebec nationalists, all your talk about the nation means nothing. I'd planted my stake in the ground on the national unity issue, and now it was time to pay the consequences.

Our opponents in the Conservative government had been watching all of this, none more so than the prime minister, Stephen Harper. As our leadership campaign drew to a close in late November 2006, he suddenly decided to snatch the initiative away from us. He introduced a motion in the House of Commons recognizing that Quebeckers—not Quebec itself—constituted a nation within a united Canada.[3] The Bloc Québécois separatist party howled in dismay: they would much rather have had their federalist opponents deny the national character of Quebeckers' aspirations. Our party howled because we wanted the credit for raising the issue. But the prime minister had us where he wanted us. When the motion was called, I rose in my seat in the House and voted to acknowledge, for the first time in our parliamentary history, the national identity of one of our constituent peoples. I'd played my part in making it happen, but the prime minister, with the tactical shrewdness that was becoming a trademark, got such credit as there was to be had.

As our leadership campaign criss-crossed the country, I began to understand Canada as I had never done before. At first, the impression was of a cacophony of voices competing for recognition and acknowledgement. Common bonds of national citizenship appeared thin and attenuated. It took me a while to see my country as the site of a constant competition among groups and interests to define what the collective "we" should stand for. Of course we had moments of shared enthusiasm for the country, but moments of shared euphoria and common allegiance are actually less frequent than day-by-day conflict over shared meanings. What a person wants from his or her national community often conflicts with what others want. Every community wants recognition of its own distinctiveness but is reluctant to grant it to others. Canadian communities often give the impression of being sealed off from each other. Immigrant communities wanted more immigration and unionized workers wanted less; rich people wanted tax breaks and poor folks wanted a better deal. Gun control, of any kind, was poison in any small town or rural district, and yet it was the key to holding the vote in a downtown core. Everywhere people wanted more federal money, but everywhere people wanted the federal government to stay out of provincial jurisdictions. The defence of the local and provincial was as strong on the island of Newfoundland or in the interior of British Columbia as it was in deepest Quebec. As these facts sunk in, I began to see our country as a political rather than a natural fact. Once you see a country as a sustained, everyday act of will, you understand why politicians matter. They bring people who want different things into the same room to figure out what we share and want to do together. Countries are "imagined communities," and politicians are the ones who represent what we share and then figure out the compromises that enable us to live together in peace.[4] Throughout that summer of my leadership campaign in 2006, I talked about the "spine of citizenship" that ought to tie us together through all our differences. The spine meant more than equality before the law and rough comparability of services across regions. It meant for government to do what it could to strengthen the common experiences, sense of shared history and common rights and responsibilities that make us into a people. It's only when you're in politics that you understand both the divisions of a country and the hunger for unity that transcends those differences. Politicians have to find ways to articulate what is common and then build that common life into the fabric of its institutions. I didn't know that this was my job when I started in politics, but I soon learned.

As we travelled the country that summer, one division seemed both overpowering and, at the same time, almost completely ignored. It was the division between urban and rural, downtown and hometown, north and south, metropolitan and remote. In the downtown parts of the country, along the American border, time ran fast and jobs were mostly plentiful. In the rural, remote and northern parts—most of the country—time ran slowly, the girl at the gas station cash register read the want ads from the big-city paper and dreamed of escape, the Internet connection was dial-up or non-existent, the roads turned to gravel on the edge of town, college was far away, and the nearest hospital was a four-hour drive. The country was divided into two kinds of places: those where you could make a living where you grew up, and those where you had to leave if you wanted to have a chance of a better life.

This seemed to be an inequality that no one was talking about—and as the campaign went on I talked about it more and more. There was nothing wrong about leaving your birthplace if you wanted to, but it didn't seem right that so many people had no option but to leave. Government alone couldn't stop depopulation of remote and rural regions, but surely it could do something—with investment in roads and schools and Internet connections—to enable those who wanted to stay to raise a family where they stood. Most of the resource wealth of the country, after all, was in rural, remote or northern areas. That was where the mines were, and the acres of wheat and forest, and the pumpjacks drawing out the oil and gas. Some of the most desolate places I ever visited—Indian reserves, dwindling and abandoned towns—were right on top of natural resource bounty. Surely there was a way to make some of the wealth stay where it was instead of being sucked down into the big cities. I became the unlikely candidate of the urban–rural divide, the hard geography of opportunity that keeps so many of our brightest people from moving forward unless they move away. It came to me slowly, but I became determined to fight for a country where hope is fairly distributed, where everyone gets a chance to build a life where they stand.

These are the ways that doing politics changes the kind of person you are and the beliefs you start with. A thousand meetings in out-of-the-way places, conversations with every kind of person, rich and poor, old and young, have a sedimentation effect. You no longer remember the particulars, but layer by layer a truth settles inside you. You take the country into yourself. You learn the terrain. What begins as an adventure just for yourself becomes a journey on behalf of others. Politics slowly introduces you—sometimes the hard way—to the people you want to do politics for and the country you want to build together.

FIVE
MONEY AND
LANGUAGE

BY MIDSUMMER 2006, I was still the front-runner in the race and I was encountering any front-runner's standard problems. We had become the target of all the other campaigns, and rival candidates were beginning to negotiate deals with each other to stop me from winning. To meet this challenge, we had to scale up our operation and get better at bringing delegates over to our camp. Our offices outgrew a cramped space above a restaurant on Isabella Street, just off the Yonge Street strip in downtown Toronto. We moved to larger quarters nearby on Bloor Street that a property developer let us use—and we just kept growing.

I did not make the mistake of trying to run my own campaign. I was too busy travelling the country and raising money. Whenever I did show up in my headquarters and surveyed the banks of phones and the complete strangers manning them, all giving me a cheerful wave, I was amazed at the sheer size of the operation. I left management to Ian Davey and a committed team of young lawyers. They had taken leave from their day jobs and were working all God's hours on minimum wage. I would rather have worked with them than any number of paid consultants (even if I could have afforded them, which I couldn't). Politicians need consultants with their polls, focus groups and marketing strategies, but they shouldn't let the paid professionals take over a campaign. Politics has to keep a large place for volunteers who come in off the street with their own talents and dreams. Without the enthusiasm of volunteers to inspire them, politicians risk becoming the puppets of their paid strategists. Besides, volunteers have a loyalty that cannot be bought. A leader's task in any campaign is to hold their loyalty and stay true to their expectations. My people stayed with me through thick and thin and many have become friends. None had ever run a national campaign before, and while I was out across the country, they were building a base of organizers to ensure that when the day came for each Liberal riding association to pick their delegates for the convention, they would be voting for a slate committed to me. Our young team was doing an extraordinary job, but our organization kept outgrowing our finances.

By American standards, the budget for our leadership campaign was ridiculously small, 2.3 million dollars in total. That's why, incidentally, we drove the back roads in an old Buick Regal, why we flew commercial and slept in modest hotels and the spare rooms of supporters. That's the Canadian way. Our democracy is relatively inexpensive. In 2011, in a country larger than the US but with only a tenth of the population, a federal election cost $291 million. In 2012, the total cost of US elections came to six billion dollars.[1] We don't just spend less, we keep it under tight control. In Canada we have put campaign finance under the supervision of an all-powerful federal agency, Elections Canada. As they do in Europe, political parties receive taxpayers' money to run their campaigns, according to the number of votes they received at the previous election.[2] Candidates get a tax-funded rebate for their election expenses and there are strictly enforced upper limits for expenditure at both the constituency and national levels. As for the leadership campaign in 2006, the maximum any donor could give me for my campaign was around thirty-three hundred dollars. No foreign donations or cash were acceptable. We had to report each of these contributions, with the name and address of the donor, to Elections Canada. They posted those on a publicly accessible website. Only officially reported and receipted donations were entitled to tax relief. Somewhere in cyberspace you can still find the list with the names of every brave soul who ever gave me a donation in my political career. All of these rules imposed demanding reporting requirements on the campaign staff, but they liberated me as a candidate. Anyone who's run for public office knows that moment at a fundraiser when some burly and well-heeled stranger in a suit puts his arm around you and gets his picture taken, leaving you to wonder whether you've just been snapped with a crook. Campaign finance rules can free you from that fear. I knew where the money was coming from and who was giving it to me, and, thanks to the donation limit, I was not beholden to any powerful donor. It also liberated the generous people who supported me. The donation limit was so low that it freed them from any suspicion that they were trying to buy influence or access. They wanted to support the political process and they liked being part of the excitement. My experience leaves me with a strong conviction that government regulation of campaign finance is essential—with strict reporting and disclosure requirements, together with an unbreakable upper limit on donations and a ban on third-party political advocacy. I'd go still further and ban political advertising outside election time, in order to put a stop to the permanent campaign that alienates voters and diverts governments from governing. I want to liberate politicians from the pressures of big money as well as the drive-by smears by third-party advocacy groups. Let them make their case by all means, but don't let them use raw money power to bludgeon us all on the airwaves.

Money is one area of politics where American attitudes and practices—recently set out in the Supreme Court's Citizens United judgment—leave me baffled.[3] No matter what the justices may say, money is not speech. It's power. It astonishes me that raw financial influence on the political process has been able to wrap itself in the mantle of First Amendment rights that are supposed to protect the integrity of democratic debate. Besides, it's not as if the American political tradition does not understand that money power can compromise the integrity of elections and corrupt the representatives of the people. Founding Fathers like Thomas Jefferson and James Madison were well versed in the classical republican political discourse on virtue and corruption that went back to the Roman republics. That discourse taught them clearly that money needs to be strictly regulated in politics lest it corrupt a free people. In an 1816 letter, Thomas Jefferson declared that he wished to "crush in its birth the aristocracy of our moneyed corporations, which dare already to challenge our government to a trial of strength and bid defiance to the laws of our country."[4] That process of corruption is well advanced, it seems to me, and a return to virtue is overdue, regulated, if no other solution is possible, by a strengthened federal elections commission with the power to require public disclosure of every dollar that goes into politics. America needs to return the First Amendment to its original purpose, which was to protect the integrity of democratic debate. The influence of money frustrates that constitutional goal. The Canadian model is unlikely to be the right one for the US, but the Canadian model, like the European ones, shows that you can regulate money in politics without diminishing one iota of freedom to argue and debate.

In midsummer, I took a break, disappeared with Zsuzsanna and sat down to write a policy manifesto. We were halfway through the campaign and other candidates were putting out their stalls. Ken Dryden, for example, wrote an impressive document called "Big Canada," a strong call for a more ambitious country. Reading it, I wanted to put my own ideas onto paper and get them into the national debate. The manifesto I wrote was nearly eight thousand words and was called "An Agenda for Nation Building." If the Conservatives under Stephen Harper were determined to roll back the state and diminish the function of the federal government in national life, I thought liberalism should stand for the opposite: for a government that would have one central purpose—strengthening the spine of citizenship uniting all Canadians. We were so spread out across a continent, so divided by region, race, religion and language, that a central government's mandate ought to be to guarantee equal conditions of citizenship for all. That didn't mean big or intrusive government—since citizenship has to mean freedom—but it did mean one that would ensure, for example, that every qualified Canadian that got the grades could get post-secondary education and not be crippled by debt; that every Canadian could move from one province to another and still be able to count on roughly the same quality of social services, employment insurance and health care. Our party, together with the New Democrats, had created a publicly funded health-care system. We had both fought to make sure that health care didn't depend on what was in your wallet. Now the battle had to focus on ensuring that access didn't depend on your postal code. Rural, remote and northern Canada had just as much right to good health care as the big cities. The purpose of national standards in health care and common approaches to our problems was to ensure that we were more than ten provinces and three territories strung out like birds on the wire of the forty-ninth parallel, our border with the US. We were one country, and we'd always understood that imaginative national government played a central role in binding us together as a people.

My campaign agenda had activist ideas on every subject: a plan for high-speed rail to link the Quebec City–Windsor corridor, where

60 percent of our population lives; a plan to help aboriginal reserves that were ready to leave the degrading tutelage of the Indian Act and create a new relationship of independence as equal citizens; a plan to revitalize federal investment in science and technology to offset the long-standing weakness of our private sector in investing in research and development. We wanted a national energy strategy to strengthen east–west energy corridors in electricity, natural gas and petroleum and to offset the predominantly north–south flow of our electricity grid and natural gas lines. My vision of how to get this done was not command and control from our capital, but partnership with provinces and the private sector, with the prime minister's role being to map out a strategy, figure out where common priorities lay and then insert the crowbar of political will at the right leverage points to get it done.

The cynics will say that big thinking is a typical delusion of intellectuals foolish enough to try their luck in politics. This fails to appreciate the decisive role that ideas can play in defining a candidate, and in bringing people over to your side. Politicians must have special gifts for knowing when an idea's time has come and for dramatizing those ideas so that citizens are gripped by the vision. When we released "An Agenda for Nation Building," we had our fair share of catcalls from the press and rival candidates, but I could tell from the way young people came to talk to me after meetings, with well-thumbed copies of our little red book in their hands, that we were striking a chord.

Thanks to these ideas and an energetic cross-country campaign, I had made the running in the race so far. Now my rivals were waiting for me to stumble.

In July 2006, war erupted in Lebanon, and by early August, all of the candidates for the leadership were being judged by how well we positioned ourselves in relation to the unfolding crisis. It is worth pausing to reflect on how peculiar this was. None of us could have had any conceivable impact on the outcomes in the Middle East. We were in opposition rather than government. At most, the issue of the war offered opportunities to appeal for votes in the Jewish community and the Lebanese and Muslim communities across the nation. However real the suffering was in Lebanon itself, it was deeply unreal as a political issue in a Canadian leadership contest. But politics is like that. Issues arise over which a politician has no actual control but which come to define whether he is up to the job.

When understood politically, the war in Lebanon was an opportunity to position myself. Positioning is not the same as taking a position. It is not about addressing the substance of an issue or producing a policy that responds to the complexity of the situation. No actual expertise is necessary in order to position effectively. Positioning is about placing yourself on a political spectrum, differentiating yourself from your opponent without alienating too many people in the process. To position yourself is to align your public stance to the constituency you wish to win over. You have to be strategic, meaning that you don't have to say what you think but you must say what you intend. If you position successfully, you win support without appearing to cut your cloth to suit your audience. If your positioning fails, you will be seen to be pandering.

To put it plainly, my positioning on the Lebanon war was a disaster. In an unguarded moment, I told an interviewer that I wasn't losing sleep over casualties in Hezbollah-held areas in Lebanon. I meant that Hezbollah had begun the war and had to accept the consequences, but my words were quickly parsed as cold-blooded indifference to civilian suffering. This did not go down well in Montreal, where there is a strong Lebanese presence. Days later, in a television appearance on Quebec's most watched program, *Tout le monde en parle* (*Everybody's Talking About It*), trying to repair the damage done by my previous remark, I said that Israeli forces may have committed a "war crime" in their attack on a place called Qana. Once my words were translated and circulated in the English press across the country, all hell broke loose. What I meant was that the Israel Defense Forces, in a legitimate response to Hezbollah attacks, had engaged in indiscriminate use of force against a target that housed civilians. At Harvard I had taught the Geneva Conventions and I knew the distinction between a war crime and a crime against humanity. I didn't believe the Israel Defense Forces had been slaughtering civilians. I believed they had used excessive and indiscriminate force. What Jewish community supporters heard, however, was that I was accusing Israel of behaving like the Nazis.

It's not what you mean. It's what they hear. I would not retract, because Human Rights Watch had confirmed the use of indiscriminate force, but I did reaffirm my lifelong commitment to Israel's right to defend itself. Nothing I said dug me out of my hole. With a couple of ill-chosen sentences, I had managed the almost impossible feat of alienating Jewish, Muslim and Lebanese groups alike. I was aghast at the media storm that ensued, the anger and disillusionment from Jewish supporters and the way the controversy stopped our campaign in its tracks. The incident revealed the strange fact that the most divisive issues in the domestic politics of multicultural societies turn out to be international ones, in countries far away. Distant conflicts make communities circle their wagons, and a politician's reactions are closely parsed for magic words of reassurance. Your job as a politician is to position yourself as the master of balanced understanding. I failed on all counts. After the furor over the Lebanese war died down, Ian Davey told me politicians have nine lives. Over Qana, I consumed eight of them.

It's worth pausing here to reflect on what the incident reveals about the use of language in politics. If you've spent your life as a writer, journalist and teacher, nothing prepares you for the use of language once you enter the political arena. It is unlike any word game you have ever played. You may fancy yourself as a communicator, but the first time you step up on a political platform, you can have the weird feeling that you have walked into Woody Allen's film *Bananas*, in that sequence where the guerilla leader changes the official language of his Latin American country to Swedish. You leave a charitable realm where people cut you some slack, finish your sentences and accept that you didn't quite mean what you said. You enter a world of lunatic literal-mindedness where only the words that come out of your mouth actually count. You also leave the world where people forgive and forget, where people let bygones be bygones. You enter the eternal present, where every syllable you've ever uttered, every tweet, Facebook post, newspaper article or cringe-inducing photograph remains in cyber-space forever for your enemies to use against you. If you find yourself explaining yourself at a press conference, you have already lost half the battle. In the case of the Qana incident, I had the absurd feeling that the missing context for my remarks was actually my whole life. Did nobody know that I had taught and lived in Israel and written the biography of Isaiah Berlin, a committed Zionist?[5] How could anyone have supposed that I was anything but a critical friend of Israel? But this was not the point. I had failed to understand how communities listen when they feel they are under attack. Isaiah Berlin and I used to talk about this. He would say, in jest, that the only real political question, when he was growing up in Jewish north London in the 1920s, was, "Is it good or bad for the Jews?" This is how language in politics is actually heard, not just by Jews, but also by any community that seeks recognition from a politician. The Sikhs wanted to know how I stood on the suppression of Sikh rights in India; the Tamils wanted to know how I stood on the brutal civil war tearing Sri Lanka apart;

Iranians wanted to know my position on the brutal theocracy in Iran. For the Jewish community, the bottom line had to be unequivocal support for Israel's right to defend itself. I had no trouble whatever with this, but I questioned whether a democratic state's legitimate rights entitled it to violate the laws of war. This shouldn't have been the issue. Why should a politician take it upon himself to rule on an embattled state's compliance with the Geneva Conventions? It was not my job. What the Jewish community heard in my comment on Qana was that I was questioning their right to defend themselves. No matter what I did after that, I could not recover the confidence of the community leadership. When Stephen Harper aligned Canada with the most intransigent of Israeli positions, I couldn't rally support among those members of the Jewish community who believed Israel's best guarantee of its security lay in a two-state solution. I had lost my standing, my ability to get a hearing.

In politics, as in life, the challenge is how you learn from your mistakes. Later on, after the controversy had died down, I gave a speech at Holy Blossom Temple in Toronto where I drew the lessons I had learned:

> By trial and error—mostly by error—I've come to a few conclusions about how I should act. In reaching these conclusions I am guided by one of Winston Churchill's wonderful remarks. He said politicians shouldn't be sofas. We shouldn't bear the shape of the last person to sit on us. We should keep our own shape, no matter what. We should have principles. So what are they?
>
> The first rule is to be consistent. I must not defend Israel in this house of worship only to betray it in a mosque across town. I must not defend the rights of Palestinians to a state of their own in a mosque only to betray this commitment here in this great synagogue. I must be consistent.

A second rule is that I must not inflame discord with ill-chosen words. I must say what I mean and only what I mean. I must not pander to the forces of hatred and discord. When I do so, I betray my obligation to unite Canadians. A third rule is that I must speak for Canada. I am not here to speak for any political group within Israel or anywhere else. It is the national interest of Canada that must guide my actions as an elected representative. In relation to the Middle East, that means striving to prevent a wider and deadlier conflict in which Israel goes to the wall.[6]

What you learn from your mistakes is that politics is a game with words, but it isn't Scrabble. No one who enters the political arena for the first time is ever prepared for its adversarial quality. Every word you utter becomes an opportunity for your opponents to counter-attack. Inevitably you take it personally, and that is your first mistake. You have to learn what the lifers, wise with years of experience, have long since understood: it's never personal; it's strictly business.

As the leadership campaign approached its finale, the public debates among the candidates curdled into bitterness and acrimony. I remember one of the final debates, in Montreal in late November 2006, when one of my rivals, Bob Rae, repeated the old charge that I had some explaining to do on the issue of torture. If not, he implied, I could not be a reliable defender of our Charter of Rights and Freedoms. I was angry that a friend would repeat such a tired canard, and afterward, as we passed in the hall, he looked at me and shrugged. "It's politics," he said. He was right, of course. In politics, there is no such thing as good or bad faith.

You can try complaining about the bad faith of an opponent to the press, but they aren't the referees. They've come to watch the fight and they want a good one. As one of them said to me, "Our job is to watch the battle and then come down on the field and shoot the wounded." Once you've been shot at, you handle all your interactions with the media with utmost care. You become strategic. You become as careful as your appearance, every hair in place, tie well knotted, suit immaculate, armoured for the day of battle. In entering politics you have to surrender spontaneity and one of life's pleasures—saying the first thing that comes into your head. If you are to survive, you have to fit a filter between your brain and your mouth. When words are weapons and can be turned against you, freely expressing yourself is a luxury you can't afford. Your language, like your personality, becomes guarded. You can still have fun. Indeed you must have fun, since everyone likes a happy warrior, but every happy warrior is a watchful one.

Obviously, a straight answer to a straight question is a good idea, and when citizens put a question to you, such candour becomes an obligation. They elect you, after all. The rules are different with the press. In the strange kabuki play of a press conference or interview, candour is a temptation best avoided. Be candid if you can, be strategic if you must. All truth is good, the African proverb goes, but not all truth is good to say. You try never to lie, but you don't have to answer the question you're asked, only the question you want to answer.

As you submit to the compromises demanded by public life, your public self begins to alter the person inside. Within a year of entering politics, I had the disoriented feeling of having been taken over by a doppelgänger, a strange new persona I could barely recognize when I looked at myself in the mirror. I wore Harry Rosen suits—and Harry himself had chalked the trousers—and my ties were carefully matched to my shirts. I had never been so well-dressed in my life and had never felt so hollow. Looking back now, I would say that some sense of hollowness, some sense of a divide between the face you present to the world and the face you reserve for the mirror, is a sign of sound mental health. It's when you no longer notice that the public self has taken over the private self that trouble starts. When you forget that you have a private realm that you want to keep separate from the public gaze, you'll soon surrender your whole life to politics. You become your smile, the fixed rictus of geniality that politics demands of you. What that happens, you've lost yourself.

As November turned to December 2006, with the convention upon us, all the advice from the team was to play it safe, to cut down unforced errors, keep within the tramlines and never go off script. This may have been prudent advice, but it had the effect of draining me of conviction. I could feel myself becoming less inspiring as every night went by. All actors, and all good politicians, have the particular brand of stamina known as "keeping it fresh." They keep finding a way to renew the role. Showtime for me—the round of delegate meetings and fundraisers—became a circus act more threadbare with every repetition. As the convention finale approached and our team, now numbering in the hundreds, was engaged in frantic last-minute phoning to line up delegate support, I found myself wondering what political life was doing to me. I had made myself into a politician, and I didn't much like what I was becoming.

I hoped none of this showed as Zsuzsanna and I toured the hospitality suites of the convention centre in Montreal, as we rallied our troops and as I negotiated for support in secret meetings in hotel suites with other candidates. It was politics in all its shameless charm. Rival candidates would sit down and sound me out about what I could offer them if they swung their support to me on the convention floor. I had nothing to offer them, since we were in opposition, but I had no scruple about playing with Monopoly money and offering them significant roles in some government to come, sealed by solemn handshakes. I knew that the same candidate would then head off to the next secret meeting to see what future offices my rivals had to offer. I knew that no deal signed and sealed with a handshake would survive if I failed to show overwhelming support in the first ballot. If I proved vulnerable, my support would drain away to the candidates who had momentum. A convention where the result is actually decided on the floor is always like this. Everyone is making bets on your staying power. Power-brokers from the Sikhs, the Muslims, the Lebanese, the Greeks, from every tribe in Canadian multiculturalism, came to my hotel suite and, after solemn conclaves and assurances of mutual respect, would offer me their delegates' votes. It wasn't obvious to me that their delegates' votes were theirs to pledge to me in the first place, and I knew that some of them were selling the same bloc vote to a rival candidate in a hotel suite down the hall.

By the convention, I had given everything I had to the battle. I was resigned to any outcome and found myself humming that Doris Day tune "Que Sera Sera." The result would now be up to a team of hundreds, working the convention floor and the hotel hospitality suites, reeling in delegates, rounding up stragglers and trying to stop defections. It had become obvious that I wouldn't win on the first ballot. I had passionate advocates who saw me as renewal, change and internationalism incarnate, and I had detractors who saw me as a Harvard snob, carpetbagging elitist and George W. Bush apologist. While some welcomed my positions on Quebec as a nation, others believed I was selling out the national unity of Canada. While some were drawn to my call for a new politics, others questioned whether I had the judgment to be a successful leader at all.

Upstairs in my hotel suite, as I wrote my convention speech with my advisors kept firmly off to one side, I wanted to slough off all the negative press coverage, all the encrusted misconception. I wanted to be free of all the quotes and misquotes. I wanted a moment of pure recognition in which all the scales of misconception would fall away and I would stand in front of my forty-five hundred fellow citizens and be seen—and accepted—for what I actually was. To be chosen leader would be that final moment of recognition. You want these things, believe me. In search of that moment, I rehearsed my convention speech, trying to find the words that would set the convention alight. When the moment finally came, I gave the speech to the packed hall and felt, as paragraph followed paragraph, a growing sense of release and elation:

> I say tonight what I have said throughout this campaign. We must be—we are—the party of hope. And hope begins with opportunity.
>
> Opportunity for low-income Canadians who want to scale the welfare wall; for aboriginals who want to live in communities where small businesses can thrive; for fellow citizens who need affordable housing; for immigrant Canadians who want to work in jobs they love; for women who want to live free of poverty and violence; for farmers who want to pass on profitable farms to their kids; for seniors who are entitled to live out their own Canadian dream in dignity.
>
> If hope begins with opportunity, opportunity means education. We must be the party that says to every young Canadian: if you get the grades, you get to go.
>
> Opportunity also means innovation. Every scientist, every researcher, every businessperson and investor must look to our party and say: those Liberals, they get it.
>
> An opportunities agenda means faith in the Canadian future, a future where Canadians of Chinese and Indian descent help us conquer the exploding markets of China and Asia.

A future where we do not mortgage our children's future with debts we have not paid off today. A future where the air is clean, the water is pure.

When governments put a price on pollution, markets respond. When markets respond and governments act, our heritage can be redeemed and our children's legacy assured.

A good citizen of Canada is a good citizen of the world. Liberals want a Canada that leads in the international fight against AIDS. A Canada that leads in the fight to defend democracy and human rights, a Canada that invests in women's literacy, primary health care and good government. A Canada that invests in its military so that we can protect the vulnerable and defend the weak.

That's why Liberals are in politics. That's what we stand for:

Hope, opportunity, environmental stewardship, international leadership.

We have always had one other great and powerful vocation: unity.

Look around this great hall tonight!

Anglophones et francophones, tous ensemble!

Men and women of every faith and race: *tous ensemble!*

First Nations, Métis, Inuit peoples, *tous ensemble!*

Westerners and Easterners, Northerners and Southerners, downtown and small town: *tous ensemble!*

Tous ensemble! I cried, and my supporters in the great hall took up the chant. All Canadians everywhere, citizens of one great country, *Tous ensemble!*

Down in the crowd were my oldest and truest supporters, the team from the Etobicoke–Lakeshore constituency. When other delegates had taken up the chant, one of my constituency people, an Anglophone, kept asking, above the din, "What does he mean? *Tous ensemble?* What's he talking about?"

I had meant we were all together.

Zsuzsanna and I left our suite and went down onto the floor for the balloting. You cannot imagine the noise, the lights, the cameras everywhere, the microphones waiting for you, the strange ebb and flow of a convention floor, the conga lines of singing delegates, the strange collective madness of the crowd that takes over a big political gathering where a real decision is being made. The balloting in the convention hall took all afternoon. I toured the lines of those waiting to cast their vote and thanked people for support. We led on the first ballot, but more narrowly than we had hoped, and stayed ahead on the second, but rivals combined and by the third, I was behind. The fourth ballot would be decisive. Bob Rae had just been eliminated on the previous ballot and had to decide what to do with his support. I was on the convention floor with Zsuzsanna and we walked toward the Rae camp. Camera crews followed us together with a surge of supporters. If Bob were to endorse me on the floor, the leadership would be mine. We had known each other since childhood. Our parents were friends. That afternoon, I had embraced his mother, sitting with the family on the convention floor. We had been rivals at university. He went to Oxford on a Rhodes Scholarship while I went to Harvard. When he was going through a rough patch, he came and lived on my couch for six months. He went into politics in the New Democratic Party and rose to become premier of Ontario before suffering a tough defeat. He was an able politician, a lifer longing for redemption. As far as he was concerned, he had earned his chance and I hadn't earned mine.

So there we were, suddenly at the moment of truth in which friendship and politics clash, surrounded by camera crews and journalists with microphones held out to catch every syllable, and the deafening chants of forty-five hundred delegates, alive to a decisive moment. As I stepped into the cordoned area where the Rae followers were gathered, John Rae, Bob's elder brother, blocked my way. He had been Prime Minister Chrétien's political confidant and manager for thirty years. I'd known John since childhood. We'd both been on the floor of the 1968 convention that chose Trudeau as leader of the party. Now we were face to face, and the question was whether he would reach out and shake my hand. If he did, that meant the Rae camp would come over to me. The leadership would be mine. Instead, he did something that shocked me then and shocks me now to recall it. He bared his teeth with the ferocity of an animal defending a lair, extended his arms, went into a crouch to ward me off and screamed, "Back!" I'd never seen a face so twisted with rage and anger and a strange and touching desire to protect. This wild, passionate, animal desire to win and the animal hurt at losing must figure in any honest account of politics. That was it. I backed away. If he and his brother couldn't have it, I wouldn't have it either. The Rae camp released their delegates and, on the fourth ballot, the convention chose Stéphane Dion, a Quebecker whose many qualities included the fact that he was neither Bob nor me.

Once the result was announced, Zsuzsanna and I made our way from the convention floor, wading through the debris of confetti, discarded noisemakers and placards, toward a hotel ballroom where our shell-shocked supporters had gathered. I stood on a chair and thanked them but I can no longer recall what I said, because I only remember a young Quebecker, Marc Gendron, who had been with us from the beginning, crying on Zsuzsanna's shoulder, and our calm and zen-like personal assistant, Marc Chalifoux, losing his composure and his eyes filling with tears.

As for the two of us, we were dry-eyed in defeat. This was politics as it truly was, brutal, exciting and risky. We had done battle and we had done our best. As we shared a meal and a glass of wine alone in our hotel room above the convention centre that night, as delegates streamed home by bus and train and plane back to all the corners of the country, we knew we had done as well as amateurs could have done. We had tried but we had not been ready. If there was still another chance, we would stay and try our hand with Fortuna once again.

SIX
RESPONSIBILITY AND REPRESENTATION

SINCE THE ROMAN FARMER CINCINNATUS left his plow to save the republic from danger, outsiders have stepped into the political arena and portrayed themselves as anti-politicians come to save politics from itself. I'd played the Roman farmer and I'd come up several hundred votes short. As I wound up my leadership bid and returned to the capital to begin my life as a member of Parliament, I had to stop playing the gentleman amateur. It never pays to pretend that you are better than the game or even to think that an amateur can beat the professionals. There are good reasons why politics is a game for professionals, for men and women who make it their lives' work. Most politicians these days start their careers in their twenties as staffers and then move into elective office in their late thirties; they spend their entire lives in the bubble of the political world. I had assumed politics had a place for amateurs but I had been wrong. Outsiders can win—Barack Obama showed how—but he won, first of all, by learning his trade through those humbling years in the Illinois senate. Then, having learned the basic skills, he set out to beat the insiders at their own game by mobilizing an electorate—youth and minorities—that both parties had neglected and by using the power of social media to draw them into his campaign. When I was running in 2006, the astonishing Obama campaign was still two years in the future. No one had yet shown how an outsider could win.

Our party had flirted with me as an outsider and ended up going with an insider. The new leader, Stéphane Dion, had been in politics for a decade. He had shown courage during the referendum on Quebec separation in 1995, debating the arguments of the separatists and making the case for Canada and national unity with flair and conviction. He had gone on to be a campaigning minister of the environment, though he had to wear the Liberal government's failure to implement the Kyoto Accord on climate change. During the leadership campaign, I had challenged him on this during a debate in Toronto: "We didn't get it done, Stéphane." My punch landed and so there was not much love lost between us. He had won the leadership by siphoning away the youth vote with a strong environmental appeal and by persuading the party elites that they were safer with an experienced hand. Now, as is often the case in politics, rivals had to become allies. This, by the way, is much misunderstood by press and citizens alike. Voters find it morally puzzling that opponents can attack each other one day and then turn around the next day and begin to work together again. Where is loyalty, conviction and principle in all this? As Doris Kearns Goodwin's book on the cabinet of Abraham Lincoln shows, parties cannot hold power successfully unless competitors put mutual dislike aside, at least publicly, and learn to function as a "team of rivals."[1] Much pride and hurt must be swallowed in the process, but sometimes, as in the case of Lincoln, rivals come to admit—how rare this is—that their rival actually deserved his status as the first among equals.

I didn't feel much rancour in defeat, but I also knew that long years of opposition stretched ahead, working for a leader whose basic political instincts did not strike me as immediately convincing. One option was simply to fold my hand and decide politics had been a mistake. A couple of days after my defeat at the Montreal convention, the dean of the Kennedy School, who had been following my itinerary in Canada more closely than I suspected, phoned and asked whether I would like to come back to teach. I was touched and surprised but I explained that my decision to return home had been sincere, and besides, the people of Etobicoke–Lakeshore had elected me as their representative and I owed them some representation. Needless to say, I had other motives too. I thought the party had made a mistake, and there were quite a lot of people coming up to me in airports saying, "It should have been you." On the strength of this and an instinct that I owed it to the people to stay on, I met Dion after the convention and demanded that I be made his deputy leader, a post whose only value was that I would lead the Opposition's attack in the House of Commons at the daily Question Period whenever he was absent. Dion reluctantly agreed because he had little choice: he was a compromise winner with a weak base of support. Over the next two years, he did his level best to keep me out of the loop, and so, for all the fine speeches we both made about creating a team of rivals, we were never a team, just rivals. But it's how politics usually turns out, and had I been in his position, I might have done the same. I was the ghost at his feast.

My leadership team predicted that Dion wouldn't survive another election, and so they urged me to wait my turn. We knew that at least one of our rivals, Bob Rae, would try again. We agreed to keep our leadership ambitions out of sight. Parties rightly punish plotters, or at least those whose plots are too public. Like a good soldier, I wiped the frown off my face and fell in behind the new leader. I applauded his speeches, gave advice that was mostly ignored, never raised the flag of discord and bided my time. Every morning in the frigid Ottawa winters, I trudged up the hill to Parliament, past the shivering drunks waiting for the Salvation Army hostel to open, and waved back at my wife, at the thirteenth-floor window of our condo. Over the next year, I toured the country giving talks to the party faithful in high-school gyms, living rooms and church basements, trying to sustain their motivation, and at the same time, my own. People don't understand just how much leaders depend for their own morale on the rank and file, on their willingness to turn out on a rainy Friday night and give you a round of applause. When you are in opposition, all you have to keep you going is the party faithful. There are no spoils of office to distribute, no legislative victories or meetings with world leaders to recount. There is only faith, the belief that if we stick together we will win together.

Besides rallying the faithful, I had to pay off a campaign debt of over a million dollars. We did it one fundraiser at a time, and it took a year of comic and not-so-comic interludes, like fundraising dinners with burly and well-padded construction bosses in Montreal, whose warmth and rough charm never quite erased my suspicion that if I were to cross them they might fit me up with a pair of concrete overshoes. Other fundraising moments gave me some inkling of what large amounts of money sometimes do to human character. One billionaire who had made his fortune in mining convoked me to a meeting in a snowy parking lot in Toronto one frigid sunlit afternoon in December. When I showed up, I looked for a Bentley or a Rolls-Royce, but there was only a decrepit cream-coloured Chrysler, vintage 1988, in the far end of the lot, and I circled it before I knocked on the window. The hefty figure in a parka burst out of the door and said, "We're going for a walk." I was dressed in my best politician's topcoat, suit, tie and polished black shoes. He was dressed for a hike. We descended deep into a Toronto ravine and he barked questions all the way down the steep wooded incline. "Why do you want to be prime minister?" When he didn't like the answer, he would bark, "Try it again. You can do better." And so it went, stumbled answer, barked interrogation, all the way down, until he pronounced himself satisfied and we returned to the car park, me frozen solid, he cracking jokes and beaming with rude good health. So this is politics, I thought as I bid him goodbye at the parking lot and he got into his beat-up car and drove away. With strange encounters like this, I paid off all my debts.

Besides paying my debts, I was responsible to the people who had elected me. Your awareness of what these responsibilities are begins when you take your oath of office in a wood-panelled room near the House of Commons Chambers on Parliament Hill. What surprised me is that the oath included nothing about the people who had voted me into office. Instead, as in all Commonwealth democracies like ours, I swore an oath to Her Majesty the Queen and her heirs and successors. The "heirs and successors" part stuck in my throat, since I think we ought to decide, when the current Queen dies, whether to continue to acknowledge her family as our sovereign. Even if we continue to do so, there's a strong case for an oath that defines the basic allegiance of elected representatives toward their citizens. Other democracies have this. For all my very real admiration for Her Majesty, I didn't believe I had responsibilities to the Crown alone. Our current oath of allegiance reinforces rather than reduces the gulf between the representatives and the citizens we represent. It seemed regrettable that I was not able to swear to uphold the Canadian Constitution and to defend the rights of the people of Canada.

After taking the oath, I was entitled to take my seat in the House of Commons. In all democracies, the chamber where the people's representatives sit is a magnificent place. It is so in our capital: the House of Commons has soaring neo-Gothic ceilings, magnificent stained-glass windows, and finely carved wooden desks with seats for more than three hundred members, facing each other across a green carpeted gangway. In the middle sits the mace, symbol of Parliament's authority, and at the top of the gangway, the focus of all eyes is upon the Speaker's chair, a veritable throne beneath the Canadian coat of arms. A gallery for visitors runs around the chamber so that the people and the press, who have their own special section behind the Speaker, can watch and report on the debates.

The first time I took my seat in the chamber it was deserted, as it often is, and there was a lady vacuuming the green carpet and another one sweeping order papers into a black plastic bag. I sat there and recalled that this was where Winston Churchill gave the famous speech in December 1941 with the line that brought the house down: "When I warned them [the French] that Britain would fight on alone whatever they did, their general told their prime minister, In three weeks, England will have her neck wrung like a chicken. Some chicken, [pause] some neck."[2]

In the Speaker's office, just off the chamber, Yousuf Karsh took the photograph of Churchill that became his iconic image, cigar and cherubic defiance incarnate. It hangs there still and MPs come and have their pictures taken in front of it.

I sat there in the chamber and thought that this was where Canadian leaders had debated the execution of the rebel Riel in 1885, the conscription crisis that tore English and French Canada apart in 1917, the decision to go to war in 1939 (two years before the United States), the pipeline in 1956, and how to confront Quebec separatism in 1980 and again in 1995. It was as if the words spoken in these great debates still hung in the air. No democracy has any health in it unless debutant MPs think of the chamber with awe and respect, and unless young citizens dream of taking their place there one day. In the lobbies off the chamber, where the members lounge about on sofas, making calls, seeing constituents or rehearsing their speeches, you can easily think you've just been elected to a gentlemen's club, but when you enter the chamber, you remember you're not a member of a club but the representative of the people. You're there to speak for them.

Every time I would meet a group of citizens in the lobbies of Parliament, I would tell them that this was *their* house, the people's house. It was theirs, I believed, not just because their taxes paid for it and their votes had put me there, but for a deeper reason. It's in politics that we define who "we" are. We create this "we" by making a thousand contentious decisions about how much to tax the people for the services they receive, how much to regulate this or that market, how much to placate this or that interest without compromising a public good. Out of a thousand such decisions, brokered compromises and deals in the corridors—many of them reluctantly entered into, with imperfect information, bad faith and not a little deception on both sides—a common life is stitched together that allows us to live with each other. We persuade each other to compromise and abide by the compromises we make. Compromise is impossible unless adversaries are open to persuasion.[4] A person like me wouldn't have left a good life in the academy to enter the House of Commons unless the romance of democracy had exerted a powerful hold on my imagination.

In my years in politics, I did see democratic persuasion at work countless times in caucus meetings when my party colleagues would stand up and get us to see an issue as they saw it in their districts. Many times, these meetings would change my mind on an issue. I saw democratic persuasion work in union halls, church basements and town hall meetings. Citizens would get up at the mike and tell me how badly this or that federal program was working and I would come away determined to fix the problem if I could. They believed in their system of government and wanted it to work. So I wouldn't say our democracy is in difficulty. It is alive and well in citizens' hearts, or at least I believe so. Where it isn't so healthy is in the place that should be the very temple of our democracy, the House of Commons. I can't remember a speech I heard in five years that was actually meant to persuade, though I heard dozens that faithfully recited party talking points. The dead hand of party discipline meant that we all, and I include myself, did not so much represent the people who put us there as represent the party that kept us in line.

It would be hard to exaggerate the hold of party discipline on political behaviour in a parliamentary system like ours. In my time in politics, my friends were Liberal, my colleagues were Liberal, my social gatherings were Liberal, and even when I got in line to board a plane to return to the capital for work at the end of a weekend, I fraternized with Liberals, not with the MPs from other parties who were lining up to board with me. It was only after I left politics that I realized, with an absurd surprise, that there were some pretty good Conservatives and lots of decent New Democrats. When we were actually facing each other in the House of Commons, we never wasted a single breath trying to convince each other of anything. The party whips had already decided the votes, and it was our job to shout down our adversaries or throw them off their stride with a good jibe. Small wonder that Prime Minister Trudeau famously said that off Parliament Hill most MPs were nobodies.[3] I'd always hated this remark because of its arrogance and contempt for democracy. The trouble was, it had the sting of truth. As for solutions, they aren't hard to envision: more free votes, parliamentary committees free to choose their own chairman and run their own business free of party discipline, reining in the prime minister's power to prorogue and dissolve Parliament on a whim. This would loosen the place up, make it less predictable and controllable, but also more genuinely representative of the people.

One feature of the democracy I saw at work in the House of Commons deserves a special remark because it is so specifically Canadian: the presence in the House of members of Parliament from the Bloc Québécois, ably led by Gilles Duceppe, all devoted to the break-up of Canada through a referendum on Quebec independence. You have to love a democracy that provides room in Parliament for those who disagree on whether to be in the country at all, who refuse as a matter of principle to speak any language other than French, who refuse to take the oath of allegiance to the Queen and who nonetheless are exemplary parliamentarians, excellent colleagues and good representatives of their people. I felt proud—still am—of a democratic chamber that gave room to a disagreement as ultimate as this and yet maintained comity and respect.

Other aspects of our democracy were far less attractive. Citizens who came to watch us at work in Question Period were in for a shock. QP is an exchange of ceremonial hostility as tightly choreographed as sumo wrestling. Politicians flood into the normally empty chamber when QP begins every afternoon at 2:15 p.m. sharp, and careers can be made or broken in the forty-five minutes of jousting that follow. Questions and answers couldn't be longer than thirty-five seconds, and no one was allowed more than one supplementary question. Custom required that at least half of my questions were delivered in French. For five years, I duelled with the government, sometimes with the prime minister in person, a sword's length apart under the eye of the Speaker, with people peering down from the galleries above or watching on cable television at home. Unlike the US president, who never has to run this gauntlet, a prime minister is questioned at least once a week. This is supposed to cut him down to size and keep him in check. What happens in practice, however, is very different. Here the reality and the romance of representative democracy part company. In most Western democratic systems, over several generations, power has flowed away from legislatures and representatives and toward the executive, the permanent bureaucracy, the courts and the media. Any opposition MP feels this when Question Period starts. On the other side of the aisle, the minister has a binder, provided by his political staff and the bureaucracy, with an answer to every conceivable question. All the Opposition has to go on are media reports, gossip in the corridors, patient digging in the Parliamentary Library and, very occasionally, the leak of an incriminating document by a disgruntled bureaucrat. The information asymmetry puts the Opposition at a disadvantage and, while giving them more resources could rectify this—German political parties have their own research foundations, for example—few governments in power have any real incentive to enhance parliamentary democracy. Their interests lie exclusively in reinforcing their information advantage and cowing legislatures to their will. It would take very enlightened leaders to give more powers to the legislatures whose job it is to hold them to account.

The problem is made worse when a prime minister embarks on a permanent strategy of bringing the House of Commons to heel. In Mr. Harper's case, this was partly a matter of temperament—he is one of life's natural dominators—and partly a matter of strategic calculation. He did not command a majority in the House and so he believed his survival depended on playing the Commons game as ruthlessly as he could, refusing to give straight answers and questioning the patriotism of anyone who dared to confront him. More than once, for example, when we in the Opposition raised questions about how Canadian forces were handling the transfer of Afghan detainees to Afghan detention facilities, the prime minister or his ministers would stand up and accuse us of being Taliban sympathizers. More than once, when we questioned why the government was spending so much on prisons at a time when crime rates were falling, we would be accused of being soft on murderers and rapists. This relentlessly partisan approach was not the only road the prime minister could have taken. He could have sought deals with the opposition parties and, given our weakness after the 2006 election, co-operation would have been forthcoming. On a couple of occasions, we did co-operate. When the nuclear reactor at Chalk River shut down in November and December of 2007, depriving cancer hospitals around the world of radioactive isotopes, we worked out a compromise in Parliament that restarted the reactor and the supply to hospitals. In 2008, when it came time to renegotiate the terms of our troops' commitment in Afghanistan, I helped craft a compromise that transformed the mission from combat to training and defined a clear exit date. Compromise was possible in this case because our interests coincided. The government was looking for a way to exit and so were we, and both of us had a symmetrical interest in taking the issue of the war away from the NDP, who had opposed a Canadian presence from the beginning. These moments of co-operation were the times I enjoyed my work in Parliament. But I vividly remember, after working personally with the prime minister on the isotope issue, how he approached me in the chamber, just before Question Period, and whispered words to the effect that I had got as much as I could out of the situation and shouldn't try my luck any further. When I asked whether he was threatening me, he laughed a mirthless chuckle and went to his seat. In the Question Period that followed, he went on the attack, signalling that normal hostilities were to be resumed.

His instincts were combative in the extreme. Within months of Dion's taking over as leader of the Official Opposition, he launched a well-funded negative ad campaign on the major commercial network featuring the exchange in our leadership campaign in which I had said, "Stéphane, we didn't get it done," and Dion had replied that leadership was difficult. "Stéphane Dion, he's no leader" became the cutline on every Conservative ad. It was unprecedented for a sitting prime minister in a minority government to attack the leader of the Opposition outside of election time. This was our first taste of the politics of the permanent campaign, and it had an immediate effect. As our poll numbers plunged, the Conservative position in the Commons strengthened: we weren't about to risk voting against him and taking the country to the polls. The prime minister's partisan ruthlessness paid off, but the price was a steadily more rancid atmosphere in the House of Commons, and, it should be said, increasing public alienation from the work of the House.

I duelled with the prime minister often enough and I have to admit it was difficult, though not impossible, to rattle his cage, to throw him off his game and to trick him into an unforced error. He is not prime minister for nothing: he has tenacity, discipline and ruthlessness in spades. He conveys the impression of having fixed and steady convictions, when in fact he is prepared to jettison any policy when it suits him. It is a rare gift to combine the impression of conviction with total opportunism, and again, as his opponent for five years, I have to admire his guile. He was a small-government man when the times favoured that, and a big deficit spender when the recession came. He was against abortion and gay marriage when in opposition, but when he got into government, he was smart enough to concede that his side had lost the culture wars. He moved with the times while grabbing his ragtag bunch of prairie populists, religious enthusiasts and right-wing ideologues by the scruff of the neck and forging them into a machine capable of winning an election. This in itself was a major achievement, and he was increasingly confident in the Commons because he knew that the MPs on the benches behind him were utterly under his thumb.

Occasionally, when I had had a good day in the chamber against the prime minister or one of his ministers, my colleagues would gather around in the lobbies and slap me on the back. If I had drawn blood, I might be "clipped" on the nightly news and I would end the day believing that we, not the government, had the momentum. If I failed, murmurs would start in the press gallery and in my own caucus that I was losing my touch, that the government was getting a free ride. When I would meet constituents just down from the gallery at the end of the spectacle, their reaction was very different: astonishment at the insults and jeers hurled across the aisle. Most MPs in the chamber are so used to the noise that it takes their constituents to remind them how raucous it sounds. Most of all, my visitors—especially the women—were repelled by the distorted, jeering faces, the taunting, the pitiful adolescent lowness of it all. Nothing in my time in politics better summed up the gulf between politics and the people than their reaction to QP. For the politicians, it was life as we lived it. For my constituents, it looked like a kindergarten out of control. The public's sense that politics is a cruel, capricious blood sport conducted in a bear pit far away may be without remedy. For that is exactly what politics actually looks like, at least some of the time.

Indeed, a good politician has to understand how large this gulf is, has to appreciate that outside the halls of Congress or Parliament, most people regard the spectacle of political combat with a mixture of disgust and alarm, fading quickly into indifference. Working with this permanent state of alienation is an important part of the politician's art. Politicians have to negotiate trust against the backdrop of permanent dislike of their own profession. When you represent the people, you actually spend most of your time trying to overcome their suspicion that you have left them behind to join a brutal game that will do them no good. You counter this feeling, as best you can, by attending the neighbourhood garden party, the parent-teacher association meeting, the ribbon-cutting ceremony, the school prize-giving: all to show that you have not delivered yourself up to the alien political world. The impossible schedules of politicians, the almost total surrender of their private lives, the way they boast of how many constituency events they attend every weekend: all this activity springs from the need to show "presence," to prove your loyalty to the people who elected you, not to the dire game played in the capital city. Yet the gulf between representatives and the people cannot be fully overcome. You and your voters do not share the same information, the same space or the same concerns. Political issues divide roughly into two: those that matter only to politicians and to the tiny in-group of press and partisans who follow the game, and the much smaller number that matter to the people at large. You can destroy yourself if you confuse the former for the latter.

The House of Commons may be the people's house, but the people are not much interested in what goes on there. We tried, for example, to make the visible contempt that the prime minister had for Parliament into a public issue. We pointed out that instead of allowing us to debate and vote on separate and distinct measures, Harper had chosen to lump them all together in a budget bill, sometimes hundreds of pages long, and make the vote a matter of confidence, meaning that if the measure was defeated, the prime minister would get to call an election. These "Dumpster bills"—disorderly bundles of entirely miscellaneous changes in regulations and legislation, some of them extremely important—were impossible for Parliament to properly debate, inspect, review or amend. We were legislators, after all, but the government made it impossible for us to do our job. It was up or down, my way or the highway, and we thought this was a flagrant display of contempt for Canadian democracy. It was also a violation of democratic conventions for the prime minister to shut Parliament down altogether, as he did on at least two occasions, through prorogation. We Liberals shouted at the top of our voices, and about a hundred thousand Canadians of all parties signed a petition to protest the shutdown, but we couldn't persuade anyone else to take any notice. When politicians cry foul in the middle of the game, voters mostly ignore them, on the sensible suspicion that "they would say that, wouldn't they?" Voters also thought, and this reflects a widely shared conception of representative democracy, that they had selected us to represent them and we should just get on with it and come back and see them at election time.[4] As a consequence, however, when we defended the privileges of Parliament, its right to demand papers and documents, its right to debate, review and amend legislation, its right to do, in effect, what representative democracy demands, the public reacted with a yawn. So instead of getting the democracy they deserve, voters end up paying for their own disillusion. They get the democracy their politicians inflict upon them.

Only a small part of representing the people takes place in a legislature. A large part of the time, a good representative is back home, "working the district." I had a storefront office on a main street in my riding and people streamed through all day long. My constituency assistant, Mary Kancer, and her team would book me day after day of meetings with community stakeholders, and I would mostly listen to the people who ran LAMP Community Health Centre, the women's shelter, JobStart (the local employment training agency) and the Daily Bread Food Bank. These meetings helped me to understand what a social safety net actually means in a modern society. It's a ramshackle, mutually competitive structure of small, underfunded agencies trying to figure out both how to expand their piece of the funding pie and how to adjust to the constantly changing dramas and needs of their client base. Being a representative means understanding how these agencies work, getting them more money when you can and listening to their stories of life fighting on the front line for the immigrants and unemployed and handicapped people they are trying to help. I came away from my time in politics with enormous respect for the determined individuals who run the social services of a modern city, who spend their careers repairing and renewing the social fabric.

What representing my fellow citizens also meant—and this was a major discovery—was that I had to defend them against the incompetence and indifference of government itself. As the son of a public servant and as a liberal, this was a shock—and also a wake-up call. As citizens showed up in my constituency office with their tales of passports delayed, visas withheld, tax files mislaid, my staff and I would pick up the phone and try to help. Every representative has to develop a staff with networks deep inside municipal, provincial and federal bureaucracies. Thanks to them, we fixed thousands of problems for the people of my district. They were often tearful with gratitude when we resolved some Kafkaesque imbroglio with a bureaucrat. Being a representative of the people turns you into a combination of citizens' advice bureau, financial advisor, family lawyer and psychotherapist.

Liberals put their faith in good government but we often make the mistake of falling for our own good intentions. The reality of government service delivery was something to see: often dilatory, arbitrary and just plain inefficient. A citizen seeking a service, after all, is claiming a right, not a privilege, but the citizens who ended up in my office often had the cowed look of people caught in a labyrinth of rules beyond their comprehension. They clutched papers they did not understand and repeated instructions from some bureaucrat that they could not follow. A few of them were far from innocent, but most were just dispirited by encounters with a government they were told was there to serve them.

They also had expectations of what I could do for them that were way out of line with my actual powers as an opposition MP. Being out of government, I had to beg favours from Conservative ministers and their staffs, and while many of them behaved honourably, a few used their power exclusively for Conservative supporters. Most of the favours my staff asked for related to immigration. Here the gulf between liberal good intentions and bureaucratic reality widened into an abyss. A country that takes in up to a quarter of a million people a year is bound to have a backlog of applicants, but our Citizenship and Immigration service seemed overwhelmed by the tide. Constituents would beg me to secure a visa for some family member from India, Pakistan or the Middle East to attend a family christening, wedding or funeral. All of these visas are granted on a discretionary basis and the decisions often seemed arbitrary and unreasonable. Our party had opened up the country to multicultural immigration in the late 1960s and we had traded on this for domestic support ever since. What we failed to attend to was that a baffling visa process seemed to stand in the path of every family reunion in our visible-minority communities. Multicultural citizenship for these communities was a costly and incomprehensible obstacle course. I remember particularly two sisters, trained nurses of Indian parentage, who worked with us to get their aging parents over from India so the family could spend their last years together. The sisters took charge of the process. They went back to India and shepherded their parents through medical exams and immigration interviews, but still no visa was forthcoming. Finally, after I made a direct plea to the minister of immigration, the parents, by then in their late seventies, were granted a visa and arrived in Canada to be met by their overjoyed children. A week later the father died. The whole process had taken six years. There was no single individual to blame for this tragic result—there rarely is—and the sisters even brought my staff flowers to thank them for their efforts. But the political implications were disturbing. Liberals like me, who believed in an empowering government, failed to appreciate what it was like to beg for visas, to queue in a government office, to be kept waiting by a computerized government answering service or to hang around a mailbox every day for a late pension or employment insurance cheque. Having had their fill of these experiences, some of my constituents wanted to keep government as far away from their lives as they could. Once the liberal state fails to treat citizens with respect, citizens conclude that the less they have to do with it the better, and the less they have to do with the state, the lower they want their taxes to be. The political beneficiaries of this downward spiral were our Conservative opponents. They offered no solution—slashing services in order to lower taxes is no answer if the services remain as necessary as ever—but they had heard the mood music out there and we Liberals had not.

In September 2008, after two and a half years in power, Mr. Harper decided that his attack ads against our leader had softened up the electoral terrain sufficiently to allow him to call an election in search of a majority government. This is a prime minister's prerogative, but in doing so, he reneged on his own promise to give Canada fixed election dates. In the campaign, we tried to paint the prime minister as a US right-wing ideologue. The real truth is that he is a transactional opportunist with no fixed compass other than the pursuit of power. In his campaign ads, he transformed his image from ruthlessly combative leader to a gentle, sweater-wearing hockey dad smiling beside the family fireplace.

The election coincided with the collapse of Lehman Brothers, the meltdown of insurance giant ICG and the worldwide destruction of savings, pensions and investments. Lonesome voices had been warning about the sub-prime bubble and the unsustainable ascent of housing prices, but no one was listening. The crisis caught the entire political class of the globe—us included—by surprise. We had been fighting our political games in capitals around the world, jockey-ing for power, and meanwhile, the dashboard of the global economy had been flashing red.

In the face of the sudden global crisis, the prime minister's political instincts deserted him and he misplayed his reaction, notoriously sug-gesting, as stock markets tumbled, that now was a good time to pick up some bargain investments. Unfortunately, we didn't have anything much more coherent to say ourselves. We ran on a carbon tax, which, in the context of a sudden meltdown in financial markets, was good policy but bad politics. During my campaign for re-election in my own district, I received an education from the voters in the politics of climate change. One woman, backing her car out of her driveway, stopped, rolled down her window and said, "I have to pick up my kid at hockey practice every Wednesday at five. There isn't any public transport out here in the suburbs, so all you Liberals are doing is jacking up the price of my gas." She was locked into a high-carbon lifestyle and she couldn't substitute a low-carbon solution, and she knew that even if you prom-ised her public transit it would take years to arrive at the bottom of her street. Encounters like this are what make democracy a continual education for any politician. This woman helped me understand that carbon taxes will become politically palatable only when we solve our citizens' substitution problems and make it efficient for them to shift to low-carbon solutions. On election day in October 2008, anxious and bewildered voters split their vote. They weren't convinced by the carbon tax and reduced us from 103 to 77 seats. They increased the Conservative seat total from 124 to 143 but denied the prime minister his majority, believing that he had mishandled the unfolding global financial crisis. Voters gave Jack Layton's New Democrats on the left eight more seats. The centre of Canadian politics was fragmenting in the face of the oncoming financial storm.

In November 2008, the leader of our party, Stéphane Dion, faced up to the magnitude of our defeat and announced that he would resign and make way for a new leader. There would be a leadership convention to name a successor six months hence, in May 2009 in Vancouver. I wasn't especially elated, since the state of our party was dire, but I declared my candidacy and set to work ensuring that this time victory would be mine. Only Bob Rae and Dominic LeBlanc, a seasoned young MP from New Brunswick, entered the race. It was down to the three of us.

When the House returned in November, Prime Minister Harper surprised everyone by failing to bring forward any measures to deal with the gathering economic crisis. He ignored the meltdown altogether and instead proposed ludicrously partisan measures—including withdrawal of public funding for political parties—that were calculated to inflame the opposition. This was astonishingly combative and ill-advised political behaviour from a prime minister who was supposed to be a master strategist. Within a month of securing an increased number of seats in the House, he was provoking the opposition and jeopardizing his control of the House of Commons. For the first time in two years, he had given us a real opportunity to counterattack. But we were without a leader. Then, out of the blue, without consulting anyone but a handful of his loyalists, Dion announced that he had negotiated a secret pact with Jack Layton of the New Democratic Party and Gilles Duceppe of the Bloc Québécois to defeat the Conservatives and form a coalition to replace them. Normally an election would follow a government defeat in the House, but since there had just been one, the new coalition partners believed they could go to the governor general, the head of state, and seek her permission to form a government of their own. If that coalition could command a majority in the house, no new election would be necessary and a Liberal–NDP government would take over. The Bloc Québécois would not have seats at the cabinet table, but the coalition's future would depend on their support in Parliament. The coalition agreement proposed a serious package of stimulus measures to pull the country out of recession. Dion published his coalition plan, revoked his resignation and announced that he would serve as temporary prime minister of the coalition government until the party reconfirmed his leadership at a convention. Nothing like this had ever been proposed in Canadian politics before, and it came as a thunderclap, especially to me. Although I was the party's deputy leader, I had been excluded from the secret negotiations with the other parties. What I saw was a desperate leader clinging to power by any means, resorting to a *coup de théâtre* to survive. It might just have worked had he been an adroit and effective performer, but he drew only laughter and dismay when he presented his plan on national television, in a performance so poorly produced and so ineptly delivered that cruel wits called it a beheading video.

It was an episode that serves to remind just how unfathomable behaviour can be in politics. Here was a principled political leader with a fine reputation for standing up to separatist rhetoric in Quebec, now making a secret deal with the leader of a separatist party. Here was a leader who had written eloquently about politics, now unable to explain the coalition in simple terms voters could understand. Here was a constitutional expert who failed to grasp that a coalition, however legitimate it might be in theory, lacked all legitimacy in reality. The problem was not a coalition itself. You can make coalitions among winners. The British Conservatives and Liberal Democrats showed how to do it in May 2010, and while that coalition has had a difficult ride since, there has never been any question of its legitimacy.[5] In our case, it was a coalition of losers. The government had just increased its seats in the House of Commons, while we had lost seats. How were we to explain to the people that we were throwing out a government duly re-elected two months before? A prime minister defeated in the House of Commons would ask the governor general to dissolve Parliament and hold new elections. How were we—no small detail this—to persuade the governor general to call on us to form a government instead? Why wouldn't she send us back to seek a mandate from voters? Would we have any chance of getting such a mandate against a government already howling that we were staging a coup? Why would voters support a coalition of losers who just months before had been campaigning against each other?

I was aware as anyone else that unless progressive forces in Canada got together, the Conservatives could be in power for a long time. The NDP and the Bloc Québécois were political rivals—we'd been fighting them in the back alleys of Canadian politics for years—but I didn't see them as enemies. Had we all come out of the election with more seats, I could have supported a coalition with the NDP alone, but we hadn't. We still needed Bloc votes to survive votes of confidence in the House of Commons, and I couldn't see how a party committed to national unity could allow its fortunes in government to be dictated by a party dedicated to breaking up the country. I didn't agonize about any of this. It all seemed perfectly clear to me. The coalition crisis was one of those moments when I positively enjoyed the drama, since I knew what I had to do.

Dion insisted I sign the coalition document, as all other MPs in the three opposition parties had done. I refused and then was ordered to do so. Refusing a leader's direct order might have blown the party apart, so my colleague Irwin Cotler and I became the last members in the Liberal caucus to sign on, but only after I had made my opposition clear. By this time, the party was close to coming apart anyway, divided from top to bottom about the coalition deal. My opponent in the leadership battle, Bob Rae, had been in the NDP most of his political life and so the idea of a coalition with them seemed attractive. He also thought we had our foot on the prime minister's neck and should keep it there. But most of the caucus thought as I did, and support for Rae, Dion and the coalition began to drain away. In mid-December, after polarized debates within the caucus, Dion realized that he no longer had the support to proceed, and he threw in the towel. Dominic LeBlanc announced that he had moved his support to me. Bob Rae then looked at the numbers and threw down his cards. The caucus of Liberal MPs and senators met and elected me temporary leader of the party, subject to confirmation by the rank and file at a party convention to be held in May in Vancouver.

So here I was, leader of the party at last, in the middle of a full-blown constitutional crisis that had split us in two. Ahead of us loomed a vote of confidence in the House, moved by all the opposition parties. In mid-December, the prime minister, now cornered, went to the governor general, who allowed him to prorogue Parliament, thus enabling him to avoid defeat in the House of Commons. By this stratagem, Harper saved his government. We all went home for Christmas to think matters over.

Over Christmas, the NDP leader and I met in secret and he implored me to defeat the government and then govern in coalition with his party. I can remember how eager Jack Layton was, how he talked about giving "a new politics" a chance. I told him that I would have difficulty bringing my caucus along. The problem was more fundamental than that. What kind of "new politics" was it when it had emerged, half-baked, from secret deals with separatists in backrooms? There was enough of a gulf between politics and the people as things stood. A coalition would widen this into an abyss. I had a very clear idea of what awaited me if I were to become prime minister in these circumstances. At every public appearance, I was sure to be greeted with a demonstration of citizens accusing me of stealing the job. We were also in the midst of what was rapidly developing into the worst financial crisis since the thirties. Opportunism may be a virtue in politics, but exploiting a crisis of this dimension was sure to earn us contempt. This was no time to test the patience of the voters, no time to assume that their cynicism was equal to our own. It was time to listen to the people when they said: save our jobs and stop playing games.

I often replay these events in my mind, wondering whether I could have seized Jack Layton's offer of a "new politics," but I have concluded that we just didn't have enough seats between the NDP and the Liberals to command a majority in the House of Commons: the coalition lacked legitimacy and stability. Some day in the years ahead, a realignment bringing together Liberals from the centre and the New Democrats from the left might well offer Canadians a credible alternative to the long Conservative hegemony. But it wasn't there in December 2008, and it couldn't be conjured out of a hat and sold to the Canadian people just months after an election in which they had sent the Conservatives back to Ottawa with more seats. So I turned down the coalition, not knowing that as I did so, I had just given up my one chance to be the prime minister of my country.

SEVEN
STANDING

IN JANUARY 2009, with the cameras rolling and television come-dian Rick Mercer helping me load a mattress off a truck and carry it up to our new bedroom, Zsuzsanna and I moved into Stornoway, the official residence of the leader of the Opposition, in a tree-lined suburb of Ottawa. Bob Rae showed up to give us a hand and everyone laughed when he unloaded our television on camera and dropped it onto the driveway. In this and other rituals we sought to stitch together our relationship and offer the public at least the image of a team of rivals. Too much had happened between us to restore our friendship, but he was professional enough to understand that we had to behave as if we were playing on the same team.

As for Zsuzsanna and me, we'd never lived in a house so distin-guished. Between 1940 and 1945, it had been the home of the Queen of the Netherlands, then in exile during the Nazi occupation of her country. In my study there were pictures of the Queen as a little girl, and every spring the tulips the Dutch government had given Canada as a thank-you present for giving a home to the exiled royal family would burst into bloom all over Ottawa. Over the fireplace hung a magnificent gouache portrait of Sir Wilfrid Laurier, Liberal prime minister, a handsome and wily master of politics at the peak of his powers. I was now the interim leader of the party he had once led and

I couldn't help but look at the portrait and feel the eyes of the old master upon me. Stornoway brought home to both of us the measure of the office I had just won. We certainly appreciated the grand old house, especially the huge screened porch with the view over the back garden, and the family of raccoons that lived beneath it. On summer nights, the raccoons would wander out into the garden, and their regal disdain as they went about their business made it clear that they regarded us as intruders, which in a way we were. In a democracy like ours, the perks of office should always be modest, but the pleasures of Stornoway were very welcome, raccoons included. In the two and a half years that we lived there, it was wonderful to come home after our constant road trips to be welcomed by Josh Drache, Jerry Petit and Expie Casteura, our affectionate and kindly staff.

In Parliament, I moved into the big office in the corner—where my father had taken dictation from Prime Minister King years before— and had my first meetings with my advisors, plotting strategy. By then I had borrowed a line from Prime Minister King, who had tried to skate his way through a divisive dispute over conscription in 1944 by saying, "Conscription if necessary, but not necessarily conscription." For me it was coalition if necessary, but not necessarily coalition. Former prime minister Jean Chrétien came to see me for breakfast at Stornoway and strongly pressed the case to sign the coalition deal and bring down the Harper government. You have to listen carefully to a man who won three majority mandates in a row, but I was surprised at his lack of concern about the problem of legitimacy. He seemed to assume the Canadian public would simply roll over and accept a coalition between parties that had once been sworn enemies. I simply disagreed. By this time, I was convinced that the coalition was useful to us as a political tool to extract maximum advantage from a government on the run. We wanted to keep the prime minister guessing as to whether we would vote for his budget or not, and thus to secure a budget we could support. In January, Harper invited me to a meeting to discuss ideas for the budget, and when I showed up in his office, I got the impression of a once-cocky leader now hanging on by his fingernails, rattled by his mistakes and worried that he might not survive the upcoming vote in the House. When he asked for our economic proposals, I told him that it was his budget, not ours, and he would have to take responsibility for what was in it. I didn't want to go into coalition with him any more than I wanted to go into coalition with the other opposition parties. I wanted to hold on to our place as the big red tent in the centre of Canadian life where fiscal conservatives and social progressives alike would feel welcome. Our gambit worked. When the government finally brought in its budget in late January 2009, it contained the largest stimulus package in Canadian history, forty billion dollars that would be spent on infrastructure investment in roads and bridges, job-sharing programs to bring down unemployment, and improved relief for those out of a job. Before agreeing to vote in favour of the budget, however, we insisted that the government report to Parliament every quarter, detailing how the stimulus money was spent. We feared that they would politicize the infrastructure money and spread it around their own constituencies. Once they agreed to this reporting requirement, which one minister later admitted did something to keep them honest, we voted in favour of the budget. The other opposition parties voted against. The coalition was dead and buried. I had no doubt that it had served its purpose. Because the government had been threatened with defeat, they had launched a deficit spending program that saved the Canadian economy from a depression.

When President Obama came to Ottawa on his first foreign trip, in February 2009, the coalition crisis that had gripped our capital for two months had barely subsided. We met for thirty-five minutes in the VIP lounge of the airport, with Air Force One on the tarmac visible through the windows and secret service agents in raincoats and black glasses in every corner. Right away, he said, "I hear you've had a bit of a crisis up here," with a wry smile. That was more than an understatement. Had things worked out differently I might have been meeting him as the prime minister. The president, newly inaugurated, was jaunty, self-assured and astonishingly at ease with his new trappings of power. The fact that he had inherited the worst economic crisis since the 1930s didn't seem to weigh him down. He knew his brief, didn't need cue cards and had a thorough knowledge of the Canadian political situation. He had a nice way of being both jovial and all business, and when I talked about the need for the two North American economies to keep their borders open and not succumb to the protectionist pressures that already were leading Congress to pass Buy America procurement legislation, I could tell he was listening carefully.

At the time, he was riding high and so were we. Our party stood well in the opinion of the country and our poll numbers climbed into the mid and upper thirties, meaning we might have a chance of forming a government at the next election. Our party was seen to have forced a government to do the right thing in a national crisis. Later that winter, when the Canadian portion of the North American automobile bailouts had to be voted on in Parliament, we lined up again with the government. It wasn't difficult: all you had to do was look at the automobile supply chain in every town in central Canada to know that we couldn't let the main manufacturing employer tumble into a disorderly bankruptcy.

It felt good to be making decisions and even better to be making the right ones. I felt few, if any, moments of hesitation or doubt, and while I found my job incredibly challenging—leading a national party, running a huge staff, managing a caucus of talented, disputatious senators and members of Parliament—I revelled in the challenge. Our office crackled with the excitement that comes when you feel the political wind at your back. My young team in the Leader's Office seized the moment to drag our party into the twenty-first century. Years in office had made us complacent. Our campaign organization had been allowed to decay. Our fundraising apparatus still hadn't woken up to the Internet era, while the Conservative government combined the fundraising advantages of incumbency with a ferociously effective Internet and direct-mail campaign. We had nothing comparable. We didn't know who our voters were, where they lived or what they wanted. We didn't even know much about our thousands of party members across the country. We didn't have the data, and until we did we were flying blind. We dispatched a young crew down to Washington and they came back with the software used by Obama's Democrats to raise money and organize their electoral base. With our "data monkeys" finally at work with the right tools, we thought we could build the competitive information base necessary to fight the next election.

The prime minister had survived, but he had been damaged by the coalition crisis. He had won the battle for public opinion by portraying the coalition as a coup, but he couldn't erase the feeling, in the press and the public, that he had brought the crisis upon himself with arrogantly partisan manoeuvring and a total failure to appreciate the seriousness of the economic crisis. Since our party had shown, through the budget and auto-bailout votes, that we were prepared to co-operate with him to pull the economy out of the ditch, we expected him to change course and become less nakedly partisan. I told the prime minister in one of our meetings that if he wanted our co-operation in Parliament he would have to call off his attack dogs. He fixed me with his cold eyes and said nothing, but looking back now, I see what he must have been thinking. He had just survived the near collapse of his government, his caucus must have been shaken by his astonishing lack of judgment, and he needed to demonstrate, right away, that he was still in charge. Instead of calling off the dogs, he let them loose. In early May, barely ten days after our party convention in Vancouver confirmed me as leader, the Conservatives ran their first attack ads. They ran two of them over and over in what turned out to be the largest single ad campaign in Canadian history outside of an election period. Their lines became bywords. If you were in Canada at the time, you probably know them by heart: "Michael Ignatieff. Just Visiting," and "Michael Ignatieff. He Didn't Come Back For You."[1]

Between May 2009 and the election two years later, they ran those ads everywhere, buying airtime on the shows with the highest viewing figures. I couldn't turn on the Oscars without seeing my face in the commercial breaks. I couldn't watch the Super Bowl without being told that I was "just visiting." Their attack exploited a hole in Canada's election laws that ought to be closed. There are strict limits on expenditures for all parties once a federal election is called, but there are no limits outside the election period. Normally, governments in Canada get on with governing between elections. They don't run campaigns against opposition leaders. But in the new politics of the permanent campaign, governing *is* campaigning. The effect of their attack was immediate. Our poll numbers began to slide. Among the party faithful I could always get a hearing, but outside, beyond the precincts of the party, a strange silence descended. I could talk but nobody listened. I was just visiting.

My opponents had followed a cardinal rule of attack politics: go for an opponent's strengths and his weaknesses will take care of themselves. In my case, what drew Canadians to me was precisely that I was an outsider. I'd gone out into the wider world and tried to make something of myself, and I'd come home because I wanted to serve. The Conservatives went right at the narrative of homecoming and turned it on its head: I was a carpetbagger, an elitist with no fixed convictions, out for myself and not out for Canadians. It didn't matter that, by the time the attack ads were launched, I'd been home for three years and won two elections. Nothing mattered. To say I was just visiting did more than question my allegiance; it also implied that I was an elitist snob for whom politics was a diversion. The ads brilliantly combined the class and the citizenship gambits in one devastating line of attack.

As they say in the States, I was being "swift-boated." In the US presidential election of 2004, some Vietnam veterans ran devastatingly effective attacks against the Democratic nominee for president, John Kerry, questioning his service record as a young lieutenant commanding a Swift Boat that saw action on the Mekong River in Vietnam.[2] Kerry had come home from that experience as a decorated veteran and had gone to Capitol Hill and attacked the conduct of the war. Kerry's testimony, which I vividly remembered because I was at Harvard at the time, made him a hero to the anti-war movement and launched his political career in Massachusetts, but it left many veterans bitter and angry. In 2004, some of those veterans, funded by a Republican multi-millionaire, launched the swift-boat attacks on Kerry's candidacy, and the attacks were so successful that to "swift-boat" became a verb in the lexicon of American politics. When Kerry appeared at the Democratic Convention and "reported for duty"—playing on his military service as his claim to the presidency—his candidacy was already doomed. At the time, I was among those who found his inability to reply inexplicable. It wasn't as if a reply wasn't possible. He could have asked, for example, why his war record was the issue—he actually saw combat in Vietnam—when his opponent, George W. Bush, used his father's influence to finagle an easy period of service in the Air National Guard, flying loops over Texas. But Kerry never went on the attack. Now that I've replayed these swift-boat ads for my students—as well as the ones unleashed against me—I begin to see why they reduced Kerry to silence. The problem was that the ads contained an element of truth, and it is truth that makes attack ads so damaging and so difficult to rebut. The ads replayed his testimony to Congress, with his lacerating condemnation of American military conduct in the jungles, the search-and-destroy missions, the killing of citizens, the torching of harmless villages. If he was to turn back the attacks of the swift-boat veterans, he had to become again the fiery young man he had once been and reclaim the fiery anti-Vietnam rhetoric that had once been his own. He would have had to say, *I was that young man and he is still there inside me. I am proud of what I said then and I believe it today. If you don't vote for me, that's your business, but I won't walk away from what I said about Vietnam.* Kerry would have had to turn America's memory of Vietnam into the same kind of teachable moment that Obama made of the Reverend Wright controversy that threatened to derail his candidacy in the spring of 2008.[3] Obama decided to own the rage of Reverend Wright and the black church of which he was a member and pivot to the question of why, decades after the civil rights revolution, race was still such a painful and divisive topic in America. In doing so, he gave himself the standing to lead the American discussion on race and, in the process, gave himself the standing to become the president. The swift-boat attack offered Kerry the same opportunity to pivot—to own his past in order to establish the authority to own the debate on Vietnam—and in this ultimate test of political skill, he failed.

I've rehearsed the Kerry moment in detail because, in the smaller arena of Canadian politics, the "just visiting" attacks presented me with the same challenge. Like the swift-boat ads, "just visiting" did contain enough truth to be credible. The fact was that I *had* been out of the country for thirty years before that. Most damagingly, the ad had included a clip of me telling an American interviewer on camera in 2004 that "we" had to decide what kind of country we were so we wouldn't torture detainees in any circumstances. Using "we" was the kind of mistake you make when you push an argument one word too far in order to win over an audience. The irony, of course, was that I knew I could never be, would never be an American. That was precisely why I had come home. But none of this mattered. I was convicting myself out of my own mouth, and the effect on the morale of our troops was immediate. Caucus colleagues commiserated at the unfairness of it all, but they were professional politicians and I could see they thought I had been struck a mortal blow.

The longer you leave an attack unanswered, the more damage it does, and if you refuse to "dignify" the attacks with a response, you have already given up. Dignity doesn't come into it. If you don't defend yourself, people conclude either that you are guilty as charged or that you are too weak to stand and fight. After all, if you won't stick up for yourself, you won't stick up for them either. This is how you lose standing with voters.

We didn't have the money to run a counter-ad campaign, and in any case, what would it have said? I love my country very much? Attack ads force you to refute a negative and drive you onto the terrain of your opponent, where you are bound to lose. They had made me the issue and I knew I had to make *them* the issue. In speeches throughout the summer of 2009, I counterattacked. Did the prime minister get to decide who was a good Canadian? Nearly three million Canadian citizens live overseas, almost a million of them in the United States. Were they less Canadian than the ones who stayed at home? Did we actually believe that the only good Canadian was someone who'd never been out of the country? I believed I was fighting for a generous, cosmopolitan idea of citizenship against provincial small-mindedness, fighting not just for me but also for the next generation. I met these young Canadians all the time: they were my students, my campaign aides, my friends. One amazing afternoon in Pearson airport in Toronto, for example, Zsuzsanna and I were waiting for a flight and, in the space of five minutes, four separate young people came up to say hello. One was heading off to Bangladesh to work on micro-credit for rural village women; another was a water engineer bound for an irrigation project in Kenya; a third was heading to Brazil to work on rain-forest conservation; and a fourth was flying to Singapore to work for a merchant bank. That was the Canada I loved, and I didn't want any of them to come home one day and run for office and be forced to defend themselves for having lived the way I had lived. In attacking me, the Conservatives were attacking anyone who had ever gone out and then come back home. And this *was* home, dammit.

No matter how I tried to widen out the issue beyond me, it didn't work. I was still "just visiting." Since the press wasn't listening to my story and our party didn't have the resources to launch an ad campaign of our own, I sought to earn a hearing the hard way. We refitted a bus, called it the Liberal Express, and throughout the summer of 2010, Zsuzsanna and I—together with a small team—made campaign stops in every province and territory. I spoke in every kind of venue: in farmyards where pigs strolled majestically in front of the podium; on wharves where the lobster pots were drying; in vineyards where the vines were ripening; and in the parking lots of coffee shops.

I loved every minute of it. The best thing about being a politician is that you live the common life of your country: at the lobster festivals, county fairs, demolition derbies, corn roasts, rodeos, backyard barbecues, and holy days at the synagogues, temples, mosques and churches. On the Liberal Express tour that summer, I served cotton candy, sampled samosas, threw out the first pitch, flipped burgers, fired the starter's gun, rode horses in the parade and felt how good it is to be in places where no one can be turned away and where we share life together. I learned a lot about the place of politics and politicians in the common life: at these festivities, mostly organized by volunteers and community groups, a politician had to know his place. The people wanted us there because we were representative of the community, but they didn't want us turning the event "political." We could "bring greetings," but campaign speeches or partisan attacks were out. What you learn from this is that the common life runs deeper than politics, runs below the fault lines of partisan acrimony and taps into our deep need as human beings to be together, to do things with a common purpose, to achieve more by being together than we could possibly achieve alone.

I loved that summer tour, especially because I was able to show the country to my young staffers the way Pierre Trudeau had showed it to me in 1968. Many of the eastern Canadians had never been out to British Columbia, and it was like watching my younger self to see the play of astonishment on their faces as they watched their magnificent country rolling past the windows of our Liberal Express. I particularly remember one small railway town, Yale, British Columbia, whose residents—all 250 of them—came out to hear me speak in the deep shade of the mountain peaks that encircled their town. Just as I got to the part about how my great-grandfather had been through Yale in 1872, about how the railway had built our country, and how we needed to rebuild it together again, a diesel rolled through, hauling ninety cars' worth of ore. The driver's horn echoed off the mountainsides and drowned out my last words, but it completed them in a way that was perfection. When the Liberal Express rolled up to our caucus meeting in Baddeck, on Cape Breton Island on Canada's Atlantic coast, in August 2010, even the doubters in my caucus had to admit that I had done everything I could to turn our fortunes around. Every time we'd made our case to the people I could tell they were listening and I felt, for the first time, that they saw me as one of their own. But you couldn't meet enough people in the flesh to counter an ad campaign that was on every television set in the country. By the end of the summer, we had made a lot of friends but we hadn't moved the polls an inch. I have to hand it to the prime minister. He didn't attack what I said. He attacked my right to say anything at all. He denied me standing in my own country.

The rules that govern standing deserve a closer look, since standing has become the primary area of combat in modern politics. You no longer attack a candidate's ideas or positions. You attack who they are.

"Standing" is a word from the law that means the right to have your day in court. Judges decide who gets standing. They regulate standing to control their courtrooms and maintain the boundary between law and politics.[4] In everyday life, we use the word to accord respect to forms of personal authority. Experts have standing with us by virtue of their expertise, professionals by virtue of their training. A friend who has gone through a tough time has standing with us. We listen to what they say. Granting someone standing is not displaying deference. It is showing democratic respect.

When you enter politics, your first job is to secure your standing, the authority to make your case and ensure a hearing. This will not guarantee you election, since your opponent might have more, but without it, you don't have a chance. In theory, all citizens ought to have standing, since all citizens are equal and all have the right to run for office. But standing is not a right. It is a privilege earned from voters, one at a time. It is a non-transferable form of authority. Nothing about past rank, expertise, qualifications or previous success entitles you to it. We can all think of people of good character who never achieved standing with a national electorate. We can also call to mind political figures whose character was questionable, Bill Clinton being a possible example, who never lost standing with the voters. Nor is having standing the same thing as being liked. We can all think of successful politicians, like Richard Nixon, for example, who were never much liked but still managed to conserve reluctant standing from the electorate. You might suppose that popularity would confer standing, but there are plenty of celebrities, pop stars, basketball players and television show hosts who fail to translate their popularity into political success. Some think that money will confer standing, but multi-millionaires recurrently run for office in the United States and lose, the most recent example being Mitt Romney. Nor do degrees confer standing. Success in education is a badge of merit that people actually earn, yet people with degrees often have trouble converting their achievements into standing. The reason is simple: education codes as entitlement, and voters hate entitlement, the way they hate privilege. Educated people routinely complain about this but they are wrong. Standing has to be earned and degrees earn you nothing. This estimable principle leads, however, to a paradox. You can be elected without education, character, likeability, popularity, degrees or a fat bank account, but you cannot be elected without standing. Given these rules, it's a wonder that we elect as many capable politicians as we do.

Endorsements from powerful people and organizations used to confer standing, but these endorsements matter less than they once did. Unions used to endorse candidates, but unions are weaker than they were and union members vote their own preferences more often than they take political dictation from their leaders. Women's organizations used to endorse candidates, but women voters want to decide their vote for themselves. When I was in politics, various self-appointed power-brokers among the immigrant organizations would come and promise an endorsement in return for some favour, but I always had the sneaking suspicion that they were pretending to an influence over their people they didn't actually have. Likewise environmental groups, the news media and editorial pages all endorse candidates and the endorsements do not confer much in the way of standing.

In many democratic systems, Brazil and Mexico, for example, political parties confer standing. Without formal party endorsement, you cannot seek election. Democracies like ours allow independents to stand, but most have a hard time getting a hearing from an electorate. Parties still retain their preponderant role in choosing who gets to stand for office, but their capacity to deliver standing for their candidate is declining. Electoral choice has become less an expression of party allegiances, held in place by family, religious or regional ties, and much more a matter of individual preference. I should know: our party had been slowly leaking members for twenty years before I arrived on the scene. The decline in the number of people who identify themselves as party members underlines a general shift toward a more individualized and volatile electorate. With only weaker allegiance to appeal to, parties are losing their capacity to deliver votes for their candidates. The machines that do get the vote out are personal. Every candidate in our party had to build his or her own machine. Obama's organization delivered the vote in 2008 and 2012, but it was his machine, purpose-built for his election, and the next candidates for president in 2016 will have to build theirs from scratch.[5]

First-time candidates, like myself, learn soon enough that party selection, authoritative endorsement and our supposedly impressive CVs do not entitle us to standing with voters. If you think standing is an entitlement, you are bound to lose. You have go to out and earn it, face to face, doorstep by doorstep, phone call by phone call.

As voters decide whether to give you standing, they listen to the political parties as well as to neighbours and family members, but increasingly they make up their minds alone in front of a computer or television screen. Instead of empowering the voter, this solitude disempowers: it increases the influence of big-buy advertising, the negative attack ads that were used so effectively against me. The solitary voter faces the negative ad onslaught alone, and if there is no one out there prepared to contradict those ads, their impact shapes how voters see you. In our response to the Conservative onslaught, we turned to mediators and institutions to defend us, third parties who would help us make our case to voters, and without exception, we found ourselves without allies. The party itself lacked the membership base and the funds to mount a counteroffensive; unions, women's groups, university commentators stayed out of the fight, concluding—quite understandably—that I had better defend myself. Few if anyone saw the attack ads as an attack on democratic politics itself.

Public opinion polling accelerates the effect of negative advertising and plays an increasingly large role in determining standing. When the polls say your numbers are slumping, you can talk all you want, but you won't get a hearing. By the time the negative attack ads had done their work and the polls had confirmed that we were in trouble, it had become a commonplace among political journalists that I was a dead man walking. I remained determined to prove that rumours of my political demise were exaggerated, but it was an uphill struggle.

Where does all this leave the voters? How do they make up their minds about standing? It would be easy to conclude that voters' decisions are prisoners of the ads and the polling firms. It's easy to think that voting itself has degenerated into a form of impulse buying. Certainly there are plenty of political strategists who try to convince politicians that political choice can be manipulated the way advertisers manipulate the purchase of a bar of soap, but this analogy between political and consumer choice strikes me as wrong. It's not just that voters are smarter than most politicians and marketing experts give them credit for. It's that voters attach a meaning to voting that they do not give to buying a skirt or a pair of pants. To vote is to express your belonging to a political community, to say what you believe in and to join in the collective act of choosing a country's direction. Voting is an expression of symbolic allegiance more than an instrumental expression of interests. Most voters know that their individual vote will not make much difference to the outcome, but they still come out to vote because they believe it matters to take part in democracy.[6] It's impossible to understand why voters in many American states waited hours in line to vote in the 2012 election unless you accept that they wanted to be heard, to count, to have their voices registered in a national contest. Those who actually turn out regard voting as a social act, one they feel an obligation to justify to neighbours and friends. They wouldn't have to justify their choice of a bar of soap or their choice of a dress, but they do feel they have to justify why they chose a certain candidate. They know that only some kinds of justification will work. You can say you bought the dress because you liked the colour; it's more difficult to get away with saying that you voted for someone simply because you liked the way the candidate looked. Voters have to give reasons for electoral choice, and this obligation to justify separates voting from impulse buying. I'd go so far as to say that this obligation to give reasons is what makes voting rational.[7]

Too many defeated politicians blame voters for their defeat. Defeated candidates will tell you that they just can't understand why voters rejected them, why their message didn't get through. Having been defeated myself, I can admit it's easy to blame the irrationality of voters. But it is a mistake. Putting the blame on voters is just a way to duck your own responsibility.

Having fought three elections in five years, I came to appreciate the rationale of voters' choices. They know their country's problems are complicated and they know that if solutions were easy, the problems would have gone away by now. They suspect that the solutions politicians offer are no miracle cure and that, in any event, they haven't got the time or the information to decide which of the miracle cures on offer might be the better one. It is rational for them, in other words, to shift their evaluation from areas of decision where they feel the issue is either moot or just too difficult to decide to areas where they have confidence in their own judgment. As the cognitive psychologist Daniel Kahneman has shown, when we are faced with cognitive difficulty, we shift effortlessly from hard questions we can't answer to ones that seem intuitively easy. Everyone has some confidence in their ability to decide whether to trust another human being, and this is the fundamental evaluation that goes on in an election.[8] The rational reason why issues matter less than personality in politics, why elections turn on which candidate successfully establishes standing, is that voters are good at deciding who is worth hearing and who is worth trusting. To decide whom to trust, voters focus on the question of whether the candidate is like them or not. The question a citizen asks when determining whether another citizen should represent them is whether that person is representative *of* them. Voters want a candidate to recognize who they are, and candidates do this by showing that they *are* one of them. Voters ask further questions, like: "Is this person who he says he is?" This is where negative attack ads that dredge up some inconsistency in a candidate's narrative can be so devastating. The voters don't necessarily trust the ad, but they begin questioning whether they can trust the politician who has been attacked. In my case, the "just visiting" ad left voters wondering whether I was who I said I was. The ad that said "he didn't come home for you" questioned the motives for my homecoming. If a politician cannot succeed in convincing voters that he is in it for them, he cannot win standing. Without a narrative that defines the messenger as one with the audience he wants to reach, no message can get a hearing.

Barack Obama showed democratic politicians everywhere how to get a hearing, when he came under attack in his first presidential campaign. His famous speech on race in Philadelphia in the spring of 2008 was actually about standing—defending his right to represent black Americans, but also his capacity to understand the resentment of whites passed over in the name of affirmative action. With that speech he established the joint standing necessary to become the first black president of the United States. His rocky path in office also confirms that incumbency is no guarantee of standing. Once in office, the "birthers" dogged him with allegations that he had not actually been born in the US, forcing him into having to make public his Hawaii birth certificate. In the 2012 election year, his opponents did their best to once again deny him standing as a real American, but voters supported him overwhelmingly, and in doing so, they changed the rules on standing in American politics forever. Race has ceased to be a bar to standing for the presidency, and in elections to come gender and sexual orientation will no longer be an issue. America and the democracies that take inspiration from it are inching a step closer to that place glimpsed by Martin Luther King when he spoke of a distant country where people would be judged not by their characteristics but by their character. Despite the victories that Obama has won, however, that country is still distant. Democratic societies that have outlawed discrimination nonetheless retain a complex code that still allows class, education and citizenship to be used to deny standing and to turn citizens from friends into foes in our politics. The best that can be said about the battle for standing is that the voter remains the arbiter. In the stubborn instinct that standing is not an entitlement but a privilege to be earned, there is hope for democracy. As Abraham Lincoln once asked, "Why should there not be a patient confidence in the ultimate justice of the people? Is there any better or equal hope in the world?"[9]

At the same time, there are grounds for concern when the entirety of politics is consumed by the battle for standing. In a healthy democracy, you would not question an adversary's right to be in the ring, or that peron's citizenship, patriotic attachment, motives or good faith. You would question competence, experience, vision, platform and ideas. In the degraded politics we are enduring, the explicit goal of attack is to avoid debate, to avoid the risks that go with a free exchange of ideas. Once you've denied people's standing, you no longer have to rebut what they say. You only have to tarnish who they are.

We can do better. I would advocate a ban on party advertising outside of election times. Let's leave the poor voters alone and confine our arguments to the halls of the legislature. Libel laws should also be used to punish the worst lies. Eventually, a negative politics poisons everyone's well. A politician who needs to unite a country in a time of crisis may find, having vilified his opponents, that he has betrayed the trust he needs to rally and inspire. If you win ugly, you are unlikely to govern well. None of us wants a democracy where elections become nothing more than referenda about standing, with the result determined by the most vicious attack ad. If standing becomes the only question in politics, none of the issues a society has to solve will get decided in elections. They will cease to be referenda on the kind of country we want. Of the three elections that I fought, none was a debate on the country's future. All were vicious battles over standing. It is striking that in five and a half years in politics, none of my opponents ever bothered to attack what I was saying, what my platform said, or what I wanted to do for the country. They were too busy attacking me. I'm not complaining, and I'll never regret fighting my corner, but the country's politics was the loser.

EIGHT
ENEMIES AND
ADVERSARIES

MY OPPONENTS DENIED ME STANDING in my own country, but truth be told, I made plenty of mistakes myself. Having voted for the government's budget in January 2009, our party developed a bad case of buyers' remorse. Having turned down a coalition with the opposition, we were now in reluctant coalition with the government. Such are the miseries that befall centrist parties when in opposition. Trying to break free in September 2009, I authorized an ill-advised attempt to move a motion of non-confidence in the House of Commons and thus bring down the Harper government. Having supported them in February, I was now trying to upend them in September. The country was in no mood for an election, and the other opposition parties, led by Jack Layton and Gilles Duceppe, who had previously opposed the government, now gleefully propped it up so that I would endure maximum embarrassment. Voters punish politicians who look like they're playing games or changing their tune. I looked like both and paid the price.

In the aftermath of this debacle, I replaced my chief of staff, Ian Davey, and most of our team with party professionals more experienced in the ways of opposition. It was an ill-handled changing of the guard, and while I was certain I had to do it, it left bitterness in its wake. I was sacrificing my original leadership team to my own survival. They were paying the price for their mistakes but also for my own. I had lost my praetorian guard and now I had no one I could be sure was watching my back. It was a lonely time: poll numbers kept plummeting, the caucus was miserable and so was I.

We had deeper problems that went beyond tactical mistakes. Once we had voted for the government's budget, we surrendered the economy as an issue. We could claim that they wouldn't have brought in a stimulus package without our pressure. We could say that it had been a Liberal government's good stewardship throughout the 1990s that had saved our banking system and our public finances. But voters rarely remember what you did for them yesterday. They're interested only in what you'll do for them tomorrow. And there, in the domain of differentiation, we struggled. We could quarrel with the government at the margins—and we did, seeking to make the absurd regional variations of our employment insurance program an issue—but with about 90 percent of the country employed, Canadians didn't seem to care much about the 10 percent who were struggling to find jobs. Everywhere I went, especially in the manufacturing districts of central Canada battered by slumping orders, unemployment and a high dollar, I met victims of the recession, but the story line Canadians bought was that we were in better shape than the Americans, and if so, the government deserved the credit. Just to make sure they got the credit, they plastered every construction site in the country with their Economic Action Plan signs. Re-describing reality so that voters believe your account of it is an essential gift in a successful politician. With disbelief, mixed with reluctant admiration for his skill, I watched as Prime Minister Harper re-described the world, air-brushing away the inequality and misfortune and calling the country into a tent of happy illusion. To put it another way, Mr. Harper described the country's problems in such a way as to make himself the only solution.

Why weren't we the solution? We were a big-government party struggling to find our way in a new era of recession and austerity. For all our credentials for sound fiscal management, we retained a reputation for high spending. This vision no longer connected with an electorate looking for relief from the economic pressures and uncertainties bearing down on their families. To address these deeper problems in our message, I convened a thinkers' conference of several hundred prominent Canadians in Montreal, with thousands more across the country taking part through our online webcast. We opened the windows and doors of the party and we brought in thinkers and writers to tell us exactly what they thought of us in public.[1] Some of what they had to say was hard to listen to. One of our most distinguished diplomats, Robert Fowler, said that our party had lost its soul. We no longer stood for anything: years of power had corrupted us. I didn't agree but I was glad he said it. Renewing the party's culture meant forcing us to see ourselves through others' eyes.

During the conference, we began to work our way toward a sharper vision of government's essential functions in a time of austerity. I told the assembly in Montreal that there were some things government could do, some things it might do, and then a few core things it absolutely had to do. It had to protect people against systemic risks and market failure. I distinguished between personal and systemic risk. In a good society, people take risks with their lives, their incomes and their ideas, and if they succeed, good for them, and if they fail, they, not government, should shoulder the responsibility. Systemic risk was something different. This inflicted harms that went beyond any individual's capacity to shoulder and repair. The global financial meltdown had devastated savings, pensions and jobs for millions of innocent people. Government had to be a society's defender of last resort against a global market system that had run out of control. It should be regulating risk in markets so that those who took them bore the consequences and weren't allowed to impose the costs on fellow taxpayers and citizens. The second essential job of government was to guarantee a safety net, so people would feel there was granite under their feet in any economic storm to come. Government shouldn't be there to take away personal responsibility, but it should be there to take fear out of common life—fear of income insecurity, poverty, loss and destitution. Finally, a government had to be there to fight for equality of opportunity for every citizen. In the new era of austerity, we couldn't afford to waste a single person, and we were wasting hundreds of thousands on the unemployment lines. We needed to invest in education, training and infrastructure to get the economy moving, and we could do so without blowing the budget, since borrowing costs were low and our deficit was under control. It was an activist vision of government based on the idea that the key to our economic success, especially in a competitive global economy, lay in opening up channels of opportunity for all our people. We spent the next year taking this message out to the people, and in town halls across the country I thought we got a good reception.

Old hands in the press corps told me that being leader of the Official Opposition was the most thankless job in politics, a seemingly endless audition for the prime ministership, conducted before three hyper-critical and restive audiences: the press, my own caucus and the public. With the press, I tried to play it straight, avoided creating favourites, stayed away from off-the-record briefings, and avoided any loose talk that would come back to haunt me. Most treated me fairly, though I don't have kind words for the journalists who phoned my ex-wife in the middle of the night in London, England, to try to get her to say I was a bad husband and father. I don't have good feelings about the ferrets dispatched to check out our modest family house in the south of France, hoping to find a splendid chateau that would fit their narrative of the spoiled expatriate. I actively despise the sheet that ran a doctored photograph purporting to show me grinning in front of a US helicopter with a team of US Special Forces. I record these incidents only because it never pays to underestimate the amazing lack of scruple in those parts of the press that are willing to lend themselves to the attack politics of political parties. I learned to live with the constant scrutiny of my private life and managed, for the most part, to keep Zsuzsanna and my children out of the spotlight. I also learned that I lived my political life in a dual world, the real world of contact with citizens who were, by and large, civil and engaging, and the virtual world of the Internet, where anything goes. It never ceased to amaze me that the same people who would never have dared insult me to my face did not scruple to engage in the most imaginative kinds of slander in the disinhibited world of the blog and tweet. As for the media, they were obsessed, as usual, with themselves, with the threat posed by the Internet to their traditional business model, but when they did turn their attention to the opposition, they treated us more or less fairly. The daily press, the ones who stuck their microphones in your face at the end of every caucus meeting, did their jobs professionally, and I can't recall an occasion when they mangled my words or trafficked in private gossip, but the drumbeat of lofty disdain from the columnists and pundits could get you down, especially if, as in my case, I'd been one myself and knew just how easy it was to scorn the fighter in the arena from the safety of the stands.

In trying to reach the public, my team and I decided on a strategy that tried to bypass the press by appearing at a series of open-mike town halls in college campuses, community centres and high-school gyms across the country. It was a high-risk enterprise since you never knew, for example, what that strange-looking man in the toque with a sheaf of papers in his hands might say when he got up to the mike, but it was a strategy that announced, loud and clear, I was prepared to listen and learn from my fellow citizens. By then I wanted to escape from set speeches and live more dangerously. Taking unscripted questions nearly every week from a live audience is the best way I know to learn the country, to know what's on people's minds, to feel the pulse. These open-mike town halls were great democratic events, but they took me away from the House of Commons, opening the door to an opportunistic attack from the NDP claiming that I was not turning up for work. But I believed in these almost weekly encounters and felt they were essential to breaking down the barrier between politician and citizen.

With my parliamentary caucus, I at first struggled to find a way to handle the large egos of my colleagues, all of them frustrated at being out of power, anxious to have my ear, always vulnerable to the latest rumour or poll, febrile, skittish and liable to betray secrets to any passing journalist. Over time, I began to appreciate the caucus's political savvy: here were men and women from every region of the country, most of them more experienced than I was, with the lifers' virtues of humour, fatalism and hope that good news was just around the next corner. We would meet every Wednesday in the magnificent high-ceilinged Railway Committee Room of Parliament, with its gigantic murals of the heroes marching wearily back from the battle of Vimy Ridge in April 1917. In opposition, it was easy to identify with these sombre, mud-spattered figures. For two hours, we would deliberate together, with some colleagues talking at the mike while others read newspapers, played with their BlackBerrys or shared whispered gossip and wisecracks. There was the usual quantity of hot air, common to all party meetings, but we all snapped to attention when anyone cut to the chase and proposed something of consequence. At first,

I dreaded caucus on Wednesdays, but I eventually came to depend heavily on what my MPs and senators were telling me. They knew what their constituents were talking about back home, what they were picking up from the other parties in the lobbies, what the journalists were whispering. There were a few dire souls—we never figured out which ones—who leaked from inside the caucus: no threats of punishment could winkle them out. By and large the caucus stuck with me and I never had to face revolts or uprisings. By then, I knew how much I needed them. When I had to rise at the end of our Wednesday meeting and summarize our discussions, I was usually able to convey what all leaders have to tell their troops—that we must hang together or verily we would all hang separately.

One emotion that kept us united was shared fury at the government we were opposing. As one wit remarked, they gave the impression of being less a government than a motorcycle gang. On the undoubtedly correct assumption that the best defence is attack, Mr. Harper maintained his grip on the Commons by constantly attacking the opposition and by using every rule in the book to maintain partisan advantage.

We asked repeatedly for true estimates of the costs of Canada's largest procurement decision, the purchase of the F-35 fighter aircraft. Marc Garneau and Dominic LeBlanc, our caucus critics, dug into American congressional reports on cost overruns and asked, over and over, when the government would tell Canadians what each plane would cost. There was never an honest reply, and in their failure to give us one they proved the plane was a bad buy for our country. Mark Holland, another caucus critic, pressed the government to explain why the cost of security at a global summit in Toronto of G8 and G20 leaders in 2010 had run to more than a billion dollars. Ironically, this was the summit where world leaders unwound their stimulus packages and where Mr. Harper led the chorus calling on Western publics to embrace the new politics of fiscal austerity. It was also a summit in which his government was guilty of unconscionable waste of public money as well as a security operation that violated the basic civil liberties of Canadian protesters. We uncovered millions of dollars of taxpayers' money wasted in the G20 expenditure, some of it sprayed into Conservative ridings so far away from the summit that it had no conceivable justification. Gerard Kennedy, another of our critics, laid bare how the money from the stimulus budget we had voted in 2009 was shovelled into Conservative ridings, once again for purely partisan political purposes. In other words, we did our jobs as an opposition and the government's sole response was delay, denial and dissimulation. Democracy can't function if the prime minister and the government withhold critical information about expenditures from Parliament. Eventually, the Speaker of the House of Commons ruled the government in contempt for failing to deliver documents relating to G20 expenditure.[2] The Conservatives' contempt citation was unprecedented in the history of Canadian parliamentary government.

We waged a similar struggle to force the government to release information relating to the transfer of detainees by Canadian forces to the Afghan security and intelligence services. Our Afghan allies were notorious for torturing prisoners. Knowingly transferring detainees to torture is a violation of the Geneva Conventions. For months Ujjal Dosanjh, Bob Rae and I pressed the government to enforce detainee transfer agreements to preserve the honour of our soldiers and the safety of detainees. The government concocted dubious arguments from national security to deny us any access to the documents we needed, and when we offered compromises, they concocted new fables. On this issue too, the Speaker, Peter Milliken, eventually ruled in our favour and found the government in contempt, forcing it to deliver papers to a special parliamentary committee.

You would have thought that contempt of Parliament and contempt for democracy would be issues that would arouse the patriotic ire of citizens beyond the precincts of the chamber. You would be wrong. When I tried to make the parlous state of our democracy and the rancid partisanship of the government a major issue, most Canadians appeared to shrug. I learned that most voters have relatively little knowledge of the parliamentary system, small patience with allegations of democratic abuse and almost complete lack of interest in proposals for reform. The government understood this better than we did and played shamelessly to the public's cynicism about Parliament by dismissing all our charges as mere partisan bickering.

There was one moment in my time in Parliament, however, that suggested to me that the public's disconnection from the House of Commons was not the whole story, and that there was also a deep yearning to see it restored to its proper place as the people's house. The occasion was the solemn apology offered in the House by the government to victims of Canada's aboriginal residential schools. These schools, opened in the late nineteenth century to assimilate Indian children, were run on contract by Catholic and Protestant churches, and to their shame, children were sexually and physically abused, beaten and scarred for life by their experiences. The schools were all closed by the 1980s, but at every visit to an aboriginal community, we felt the weight of the traumatic memories they had left in their wake. When Zsuzsanna and I visited the Stó:lō nation, a BC Indian community on the banks of the Fraser River, one of the elders told us, in a halting voice, about her experience of the residential schools and concluded, with a sad shrug, "How can you expect any of us to send our children away for education?" Successive governments, including our own, had tried to overcome this legacy. It is to the prime minister's credit that he hammered out a financial settlement to the residential schools claims and arranged for a ceremony of apology in the House of Commons in June 2008. Representatives from the aboriginal peoples took their seats in the main aisle of the House of Commons and the galleries were packed with people from aboriginal communities across the country, many of them in the ceremonial dress of their tribe. Solemn speeches were given by the prime minister and by the aboriginal leaders on the floor of the House, but I don't remember them well. What I recall vividly were the people in the gallery, leaning forward, the intensity of their attention investing the occasion with resonance and emotion. Afterward, when the ceremony concluded, aboriginal families streamed out across the lawns of Parliament and I talked with them, sat in their circles on the grass and listened as they talked about what the event in Parliament had meant to them: recognition and the promise of a new beginning. There was something moving—and also poignant—about the seriousness with which we took the occasion, especially since aboriginal Canadians have been deeply ambivalent about their political membership in our country. They were not accorded the vote in federal elections until 1960, and to this day they vote more frequently in their tribal elections than in national ones. Yet here they were in huge numbers, affirming their desire to have their historical sufferings recognized in Parliament. Those of us who worked in the House had become so habituated to the partisan bloodletting in the place that it came as a surprise to see Canadians reminding us what our Parliament was supposed to be for. The final irony of that day of apology is worth remembering as well. Since that June day in 2008, with its promises of renewal, precious little has happened. Aboriginal Canadians—and Canadians in general—are still waiting for their politicians to live up to the promise of that moment.

Apart from this one moment, when we came together to remember and rededicate ourselves, a widening gulf separates citizens and politicians. The gulf is over the issue of partisanship. From a politician's point of view, partisanship is the essence of politics. You join a team, choose your leader, issue a platform and then march forth to do battle with the other side. Partisanship means putting party line first and personal judgment second. Loyalty is the moral core of partisanship, the value that trumps all others.[3] Once you become a partisan, you enter an information bubble of political positioning. You abjure the other side, do not keep company with them, and define them as everything you oppose. Partisanship defines the world you take as normal. As I've said, I had no friends on the other side during my time in politics. We never ate, drank or talked with people on the government benches. If you were found talking to someone on the other side while walking on the treadmill in the parliamentary gym, for example, rumours would start that you were thinking of crossing the aisle. In retrospect, this seems crazy. Had Liberals fraternized with New Democrats in our minority parliaments, coalition might have been less of a leap into the dark, but at the time, I felt uncomfortable about fraternizing with adversaries. In former times, so the old hands would tell me, members from opposing parties would dine or drink together when sessions ran late, and these rituals of conviviality reinforced the rules of civility inside the chamber. Nowadays, partisanship has degenerated from the rough-and-tumble jousting of former days to really venomous character assassination. From a politician's point of view, partisanship is not some excess or disorder of politics. "Differentiation" is the nature of the business. The people deserve a choice and it is the job of a politician to present that choice in clear and necessarily stark terms. Dramatizing the choice, presenting it in shades of black and white, is essential if you hope to rouse voters from their state of grey on grey. If a politician fails to be partisan, fails to stick up for his team's ideas and starts freelancing his own line, he's not a politician, he is a fool.

When seen from the outside, however, partisanship is what poisons politics for the public. The bitter exchanges seem to have nothing to do with them or their interests. For many voters, partisan politics is a hypocritical show conducted for the exclusive benefit of the political class. It was striking, at ribbon-cuttings, dedications and other public events, how we politicians introduced our colleagues so fulsomely, effectively turning these gatherings into a High Mass of self-congratulation. When plaques were unveiled or foundation stones were laid, we politicians jostled to be in the shot and made sure our pictures made the local papers. These are the sorry scenes that lead voters to shake their heads and conclude: "They're only in it for themselves."

Voters also tell you that they hate the partisanship because it's so insincere. They can't believe what politicians say because politicians don't appear to believe it themselves. Certainly, the voters are not wrong about this. Partisanship puts a premium on loyalty over honesty, repeating party mantras at the expense of sticking up for what you believe. Every politician who has ever lived has had to sell some snake oil. For those who believe the essence of the political vocation is to speak truth to power, hypocrisy is morally repellent. But it is often necessary. In the best lecture ever given about politics, "Politics as a Vocation," delivered in 1919 by the German sociologist Max Weber, he said those who choose truth over loyalty are practising "an ethic of ultimate ends."[4] There will always be those who set their compass by such an ethic, but their careers in politics are likely to be short. Against an ethic of ultimate ends, Weber posited "an ethic of responsibility" that focuses duty on the question To whom am I responsible? If the answer is the voters, you can't accomplish anything for them if you value your conscience more highly than you value their interests.

Many of the voters I met, especially young ones, believed that politics ought to be true to the ethic of ultimate ends. I came to believe that my own conscience mattered, but party unity mattered more if we were to get power. Without power, we could do nothing. But there was a clear limit to what power could demand of you. You couldn't afford to forget what the truth actually was, and if you did, you risked becoming a hack. Most politicians don't knowingly turn themselves into hacks. You try to hold on to to your true shape as best you can, but there's no possibility of keeping it altogether in the compromises politics forces upon you. My staff and I constantly debated, for example, whether we should take the "high road" or the "low road" in replying to the constant adversarial barrage from the other side, and sometimes, truth be told, we let ourselves get down in the mud with our opponents. Needless to say, when we did, we came up looking as soiled as our adversaries.

All the same, the cynical charge, so often made against politicians, that they invariably choose expediency over principle, is simply untrue. I took positions as leader of the party that I thought were right even though they cost us votes. It was right to come out against the export of asbestos, since its uncontrolled use can be lethal, even though the position cost us seats in towns that mined it, like Asbestos, Quebec. It was right to defend gun control against Conservative attempts to dismantle it, though our position cost us seats in northern and remote communities. When I persuaded my good friend Larry Bagnell, member of Parliament for the Yukon, to vote in favour of gun control, there were tears in his eyes when he rose in the chamber to cast his vote; he knew full well that his vote might cost him his seat. And, in the event, it did. It was right for our party to refuse to vote for more mandatory minimum sentences and more prisons; on crime issues, we chose the politics of evidence ahead of the politics of fear. But it cost us votes. So if partisanship is the essence of politics, partisan interest did not always prevail. Indeed, if it had, we might have been more successful.

I learned that you can't take refuge in moral purity if you want to achieve anything, but equally, if you sacrifice all principle, you lose the reason you went into politics in the first place. These are the essential dilemmas of political life, but they are what make politics exciting. You can't achieve anything unless you put yourself in harm's way. Sometimes, I felt that voters' impatience (especially among younger voters) with the necessary compromises of political life was a little easy and their disgust with politicians an excuse to justify their own failure to step up and get involved.

A further dilemma that voters often failed to understand is that politicians who actually want to win power have to face both ways at once. To solidify their base, they have to be partisans. Red meat must be thrown to the hounds. At the same time, the politician has to reach beyond the partisan corral to those floating voters who want to be spoken *to*, not spoken *for*. A good politician has to be simultaneously in the battle and above the fray. A great old Scottish politician once put it this way: "A man who can't ride two bloody horses at once has no right to a job in the bloody circus."[5]

If partisanship were only a circus trick—riding two bloody horses at once—the worst that could be said is that it is a poor show. But the voters' problem with it runs deeper. Partisanship divides an already divided society and turns adversaries into enemies. An adversary has to be defeated, while an enemy must be destroyed. You cannot compromise with enemies. With adversaries compromise is possible. An adversary today can become an ally tomorrow. In my time in politics, I served in Her Majesty's Loyal Opposition. The word "loyal" defines opposition as a legitimate function in any democracy worth the name. Governments ought not to question the loyalty of those who oppose them, though the government I faced did so continually. They treated us not as adversaries, but as enemies. Democracy depends on persuasion, on the idea that you might be able to win over an adversary today and turn him or her into an ally tomorrow. In the politics we have now, persuasion is dying. In parliamentary democracies and republican legislatures alike, votes are decided in advance and nothing turns on persuasion, on attempts to reach out across the aisle. Party discipline eliminates the need to persuade and hence the incentive to be civil. When persuasion doesn't come into democratic debate, exchanges become pointless displays of venom. Nothing lowers a citizen's estimate of democracy more than the sight of two politicians hurling abuse at each other in an otherwise empty chamber, but this is now a common sight in legislatures around the world. As power ebbs away from legislatures and accrues steadily to the executive and the bureaucracy, debate within democratic chambers becomes both unpleasant and meaningless. Democratic peoples have reason to fear this double phenomenon—waning legislative democracy and heightened partisanship—because taken together they weaken one of democracy's crucial functions: to keep adversaries from becoming enemies.

The cure lies in civility, but civility is more than politeness. It's the recognition that your opponent's loyalty is equal to your own just as his good faith is equal to your own. This recognition does not preclude adversarial competition, even a tough punch or two, but it proceeds from a shared understanding that democracy, properly speaking, is the politics of adversaries. Against this, we increasingly have the politics of enemies. In this perversion of the game, politics is modelled as war itself. The aim is not to defeat an adversary but to destroy an enemy by denying them standing. We need to attend carefully to where all the loose macho talk about politics as war can lead. War, Carl von Clausewitz said, was the continuation of politics by other means, but politics is *not* the continuation of war.[6] It is the alternative to it. We care about politics, defend it, seek to preserve its vitality, because its purpose is to save us from the worst.

Our Conservative opponents had little originality but all the ferocity born of thirteen frustrating years in opposition. They had borrowed the entire playbook of negative attack from their American republican counterparts, together with the mental world that went with it: politics as war and adversaries as enemies. The war metaphor has insidious effects: it legitimizes a "take no prisoners" approach. War talk provides the standard justification for the black arts of negative advertising. Negative advertising certainly works, but it turns ordinary people off politics, reinforces the gulf between the people and the political class and makes it ever more difficult for political leaders to rally, inspire and motivate. Negative advertising poisons the well of politics, kills the trust between governors and governed on which good government depends.

Turning an adversary who must be defeated into an enemy who must be destroyed also has the effect of defining compromises and deals—the humble trade plied in most democratic legislatures—as betrayal or treachery. Once compromise is defined as betrayal, democratic systems become unworkable.[7] No true politician can afford to make eternal enemies. He needs to turn adversaries into allies if he is to do the job that democracy demands.

Of course there are limits to compromise, and political leaders must know where the blurry line lies that separates an honourable from a dishonourable compromise.[8] Politicians must have the spine to know that not every principle can be traded for the sake of a deal. At some point an adversary will demand something that threatens a vital interest; at some point they may even take an action that raises questions about their respect for the rules of the game itself. At this point, to compromise is to appease.

By early 2011, the Conservative government's new budget was looming and it was becoming apparent that voting to sustain the government in office had become impossible. Twice the Speaker had sanctioned the government for contempt of Parliament, an unprecedented event in the history of our country. To roll over and pass their next budget would have been an act of appeasement. There would have to be an election, whether or not it was the right time for us.

When the election call finally came in March 2011, deep inside, in that place of repose that any politician has to find within himself, I felt ready. My apprenticeship was over. It was time to show what I was made of. I remember the thirty-five days of the campaign as being the happiest time in my political life. We had a plane, a team on the ground and in the air, and our campaign machinery seemed to hum with efficiency—perhaps because I had left the logistics to a team I trusted. I had a platform I passionately believed in. It put the focus on equality of opportunity for every citizen. We were going to make sure that the Cree kid from the reserve would actually finish community college. We were going to guarantee that a doctor would see the woman who had waited six hours in a hospital corridor. We were going to make sure that every working family could afford a college education for their children. We wanted care in the home for families crushed by the burden of Alzheimer's disease. We were going to pay for our promises by pushing Pause on corporate tax breaks. We were also going to go after tax breaks for high-end people holding stock options. Income should be taxed as income, however it was earned, and these high earners were getting a break to the tune of $650 million. It wasn't about punishing success; it was about fairness. We launched the platform in an Ottawa gymnasium in front of an enthusiastic crowd, and a live Internet feed carried it across the country. For the first few weeks of the campaign, we were flying high. For the only time in my political life, I felt in full command of my message, my troops and my destiny. When I look back now at a book of photographs from that campaign, taken by a young photographer, Georges Alexandar, I'm smiling in every shot: waving from the top steps of our campaign plane, diving into packed halls to shake hands, striding up and down on stage with a mike in my hands, my face lifted up by the reaction of the crowds. From the photographs, you'd never imagine how it all turned out.

Each day concluded with a rally, and the rally always began with me warming up in the green room. I would pace about getting the blood to flow, hopping back and forth on my feet like a fighter. I know, it's not what you'd expect, but by then I understood how physical politics is, how important it is to get your blood flowing, to keep the pace up, to generate some electricity in the hall. From backstage, I could hear the noise building, and I would be alone with Zsuzsanna, taking a last swig of water and trying to ride the rush of adrenaline. Then the music would start up and out we would go into "the tunnel of love," the crowd parting as the advance team moved forward in a low crouch in front of me, moving the cameras back and leading me toward the riser, where I would stride out and wave, and take the mike in my hands. In front of me were hundreds, sometimes thousands of uplifted faces, and I'd always notice the young parents with children on their shoulders, because their kids seemed to be floating on top of the crowd.

Down in front there were the ones in wheelchairs, with their care-givers behind them. In between, craning their heads to get a better look, would be the volunteers, the door-knockers, phone-bankers, the grassroots without whom a party cannot function: retired ladies, old guys in windbreakers, kids from the local colleges, collections of Sikh taxi drivers at some venues, Hindu truck drivers at others, Chinese or Filipino hotel workers. I'd look out and sometimes I'd say: *Look around you. Look at this crowd. Feel your strength. The whole country is in this room.* Some nights it was the Knights of Columbus Hall, or the Veterans Hall, or the Centennial Lounge, the Polish Club, the Casa Italia, or even Harry's Pub. Other days we were in high-school gymnasiums or low-ceilinged hotel ballrooms, with waiters in their white shirts and bow ties listening at the back. There was something immemorial about the campaign. It was politics, old style. The campaign crew may have been tweeting at the back, but up front I could have been wearing a frock coat and standing on a soapbox. Were we continuing a grand tradition or assisting at its last rites?

There was always a flag behind me on the stage, and in some big venues I'd have a runway extending out into the crowd so that the people could get close and I could shake their outstretched hands. On a good night—and there were lots of those—I could feel that people were more than listening: they were adding a momentum of their own. Complicity flowed between us, so I felt that we were helping each other reach the next plateau at the same moment. By then I had gotten rid of the lectern, taken off the jacket, shed my professorial tics, stopped trying to be clever and tried to reach inside to the simple core of my beliefs, so that together we could reach a moment of pin-drop attentiveness where the message could get through. One night in the packed hall of a northern town, as I talked about the government and its aggressive and partisan contempt for our institutions, I remembered a line from a Bruce Springsteen song, "My City of Ruins." *Rise up*, I said. *Rise up*, the crowd replied, and soon everybody was saying it. *Rise up*. It became a call and response at every meeting. For a moment there, we thought we had caught a wave.

We were "working the base," firing them up so they'd be there when we needed them, to write us a cheque, man the phone lines, knock on the doors when election day rolled around. By then we had worked the terrain so often I recognized the old hands. I'd point at them from the riser and they'd wave back. Afterward, they'd crowd around and I could feel they believed that we could win. When they felt it, I felt it too.

Sometime during the campaign, I visited the editorial offices of *La Presse* in Montreal to explain our platform. Lysiane Gagnon, an influential columnist, listened and then turned to me and said in a queenly tone, "But Mr. Ignatieff, politics is not social work." Our platform wasn't social work: we thought investing in our people was the key to keeping ahead of the new giants, China, India, and Brazil. That was the master idea: bearing down on inequality, making sure nobody was left behind so we'd *all* get ahead. And we believed that we could shape the future instead of being shaped by it, that we could unite people, not divide them, and that we could hand the country over to the next generation in better shape than we found it.

People who'd never been to a political meeting before came out to hear us. I remember a tall, rail-thin man of about sixty years of age in jeans and a cowboy hat in a northern town, Sudbury I think it was, who got up after I had finished talking about our plan for home care and told the crowd that he had been driving a rig for thirty years and had to come off the road because his wife began forgetting everything. There was no one else but him to keep her from wandering out of the house. Your plan, he said, would help me. That's what I believe, he said, and he sat down. I never felt more validated in my whole life in politics. People like him were who I wanted to be prime minister *for*.

The press was on the plane with us and we talked to them and took questions every day, without, I'm happy to say, making one of those gaffes that can cost you an election. One of the younger reporters told me later that our campaign was the kind of political experience she went into journalism to cover. The prime minister kept the press behind a rope line and locked them into a kind of bondage relation that left them cowed and dispirited. He is a strong strategist but a weak campaigner and I was struck by how little he had to say that was positive or inspiring. His campaign raised one lurid spectre after another: fear of economic ruin, crime, immigrants, foreigners, expatriates and strangers, fear of the future, if they weren't returned to power. I just couldn't take it seriously, though I should have done. They certainly knew how to play upon resentment. They ran ads sneering at my education. A college degree these days may only land you in the unemployment line. But that wasn't the point. The point was to portray us as Liberal elitists to people who'd never had a decent education and as tax-greedy hypocrites to people who had. Resentment is the master invalidator and there is so much resentment to go around, in societies as unequal as ours, that it can be attached to almost anybody if an opponent spends enough money to stick it there. I wasn't about to make class war on "the wealth creators" and "the job creators," but I did think the middle-class families I saw were slowly losing ground and deserved some help. What is liberal politics but the faith that some forms of hopelessness and fear can be beaten only if we fight them together? It's wrong that a family has to be bankrupted by nursing an incapacitated relative at home. It's wrong for families to be crushed by unemployment and illness and drug costs. It's wrong that so many people still feel a decent education is beyond their reach. The very idea of a good country is that all of these good things should be within the reach of anyone prepared to work for them. Our master thought was that a liberal politics exists to take the fear out of our common life. I believed we were striking a chord, at least with those who had experienced that kind of fear in their lives.

I was wrong. Nothing we said, no matter how devoutly we believed it, made any difference. I look back now at those huge crowds, those great nights, and I see that we were just talking to ourselves. Our party became an echo chamber: all we were hearing was the sound of our own voices. I bet on fixed allegiance, on memory, on loyalty to what we had done. I bet wrong. Political allegiance is no longer a tradition: it's just a preference, and it can change faster than a blink of an eye. I thought we could count on a third of our people as our base. They'd vote for us if we gave them a half-decent reason. We learned that our base was no larger than one in five of our people.

We thought we needed policy and platform. We thought we needed organization and candidates. We thought we should at least show up, even if we didn't have much chance of winning in some places. It didn't turn out that way. One of our candidates eventually lost to a young NDP woman who thought she had so little chance of winning that she spent some of the campaign on holiday in Las Vegas.

I had a too literal understanding of everything. I thought I was in an election. We were in a reality show. I thought content mattered. I thought the numbers in a platform should add up. Ours did and theirs didn't. None of it mattered. It was a case of parallel universes. We were in one, our adversaries were in another, and the voters were in yet another. The winner was the one who understood this first, who crossed over into the voters' world and won ninety seconds of their attention. That was all the time any of us were going to get. Our adversaries did get there first, with millions of dollars to fill those ninety seconds with ads that repeated, over and over, that I was just visiting. I wasn't in it for them. They had understood a basic reality of the new era of the permanent campaign better than we had. We began our campaign in March 2011. They had begun theirs two years earlier.

On the last weekend of the election, a caucus colleague of mine, Scott Brison, fighting to hold his seat in rural Nova Scotia, told me he kept running into people who had been his supporters and were now saying that they wanted to vote for him as usual, but their problem was that I was an American. That was what they were hearing on the TV every night.

Fortuna also played a decisive part in the result. Jack Layton, the leader of the New Democratic Party, had been waging a brave battle against prostate cancer for about a year before the election. When I last saw him in the lobby of the House of Commons, he was pale, sweating profusely and levering himself past on crutches, because his hip had just fractured, but still smiling a gallant smile. At the beginning of the election, it was widely rumoured that the cancer had spread, but he assured the press and public that he was just fine. He began the campaign struggling to complete his day, but as the weeks went on, he reached inside and tapped a reservoir of charm, energy, humour and enthusiasm. By the end he was waving his stick in the air to crowds that grew by the day, drawn by his courage, his *joie de vivre* and his combativeness. His long service in the Commons made him a familiar figure and an alchemy began to take place, transforming him from just another politician to "Jack," everybody's favourite Canadian, a symbol of hope for everyone who's ever had to face cancer. His transformation in the campaign was an astonishing achievement, and it is not disparaging it to say that it was made possible by a masterful display of political guile. In Quebec, he parlayed his Montreal roots into breakthrough support for his party, cemented by his neat way of saying one thing in Quebec and another in the rest of Canada. In Quebec he said he would accept a simple majority vote if Quebeckers wanted to secede; in the rest of Canada he said even a majority vote would require further negotiation. We argued that it was wrong to say one thing in one part of the country and another in another, especially on an issue as important as national unity, but by then the crowds were moving toward Jack and no one was listening to a word we said.

I'm not sure when I knew the tide was turning against us. Certainly, my chief of staff, Peter Donolo, must have known what our overnight polling was saying, but he didn't tell me and I didn't want to know. It was too late to change our strategy anyway, and I was having too much fun preaching to the converted in those crowded halls. I do remember realizing that the two national debates on television, one in French, the other in English, did not do me any good. Looking back I see now that we became so consumed by the run-throughs of our mock debates that we failed to settle on a basic strategy. This was, after all, my one chance to show most Canadians that I wasn't just visiting, and my one opportunity to show some charm and warmth. Instead, I jabbed at Mr. Harper relentlessly and probably came across as just another of those angry partisan politicians. Jack Layton had done three national debates and he knew better. He smiled a lot, waited for his moment, and when I jabbed at Harper for demeaning our democracy, he jumped in and pointed out my attendance record in the House, adding that if I was campaigning for a promotion, I ought at least to show up for work. He knew that I'd been doing open town halls across the country, but the blow landed. What I remember best about the debates was afterward, in the green room, hearing the cheer as the prime minister returned to his dressing room next door. The spectacle of Jack taking me apart was music to Conservatives' ears. The visceral roar through the partition wall told me all I needed to know about how the debate had actually gone.

On May 1, we waited for the results in a suite in a Toronto hotel. A certain expectant gloom had settled in, but we had no idea what we were in for because none of the experts had any idea what was coming. The earthquake began in Quebec. The vote for the separatist Bloc Québécois collapsed; its leader, Gilles Duceppe, went down to defeat in his own riding. Their nationalist pro-Quebec vote flowed overwhelmingly to Jack Layton's NDP. Québécois voters had not forgiven the Liberals for the scandals of the 1990s and so the federalist, pro-Canada vote in Quebec also went to Jack. In the last weekend before the election, the NDP wave in Quebec, by then widely anticipated, set off a counter-wave of people fearful of the NDP surge. Instead of flowing to us, this counter-wave flowed to the Conservatives. In riding after riding, the Liberal vote was pulled apart from both sides: increases in the NDP vote pushed support to the Conservatives, while increases to the Conservative vote drained votes away from us. Our seats began falling like ninepins. I sat, with stunned staff, watching the returns on TV as the centre of our politics, the place where my party had positioned itself for a century, collapsed in one night. By late in the evening, it was apparent that I would even lose my own seat.

By midnight, I was up at the podium in an emptying ballroom in front of a diminishing band of disconsolate and shocked supporters, thanking all of those who had stood with me for five years. All I could think of saying—you cannot prepare for such events—is that failure is a great teacher and I would learn all its lessons.

The defeat was certainly a rejection of me—I could handle that—but it was so much more, a rejection of some fine and devoted members of Parliament, some excellent candidates and a century's worth of political tradition. I knew that it would take us a long time even to understand what had happened. As Zsuzsanna and I traversed an empty ballroom filled with the detritus of defeat and returned alone to our hotel suite, I was shaken but also calm. So this was politics, I thought. If you didn't understand that you could lose everything, you didn't understand what politics truly was.

There is one moment the next morning that I want to recall, a moment that shows the other side. As we left our hotel suite, crossed the lobby and prepared to enter the bus taking us to the airport, there was a single figure standing outside waiting for us. It was the turbaned owner of the car company whose dispatcher hut I had visited in my first week in politics five years before. He had been there from the first moment, and he was there, at the very last, wearing another of his magnificent turbans, elegant as always. This time, tears were streaming down Baljit Sikand's face.

NINE
WHAT THE TAXI DRIVER SAID

ZSUZSANNA AND I RETURNED to Stornoway and disconsolately packed up our things. I remembered a photograph I'd seen of men in overalls carting belongings into a moving van at the back of 10 Downing Street after Margaret Thatcher defeated James Callaghan in 1979. The arrival of the moving van is as momentous a symbol of the sovereignty of the people as the moment when a leader takes the oath of office. Now the moving vans were at our back door. The people had told us to pack our bags. In an emptying house that had once felt like home, I pulled my books off the library shelves as the portrait of Laurier, our greatest prime minister, seemed to follow me with its eyes. Every leader of the party but two had become prime minister. Now I had become the third leader to fail.

The day before I'd had an airplane, a security detail, a staff of a hundred, a car and driver, a chef and housekeeper to welcome us home, and, most valuable of all, a political future. The day after, that future had vanished. I was unemployed and five and half months short of eligibility for the pension that usually goes with six years of service as an MP. I was filling boxes while making phone calls to find myself a job. Rob Prichard, a friend of thirty years, came to the rescue, and after he'd made a few calls to John Fraser, master of Massey College, David Naylor, the president of the University of Toronto, and Janice

Gross Stein, director of the Munk School of Global Affairs, I was back in my old life, teaching human rights and politics once again. Finding a new start was much harder for many of my defeated colleagues.

I hadn't driven for five years, and so I went to renew my licence the day after the defeat. The photograph they took that day shows a person I now barely recognize: defeated, disconsolate and forlorn. The eyes—my eyes—don't focus.

I cleared out the desk in my office on Parliament Hill and bade farewell to a shocked caucus, now reduced to less than half its size. It was terrible to commiserate with defeated colleagues, many of whom had been excellent, even self-sacrificing members of Parliament and who now, like me, were struggling to comprehend defeat. Some vowed to "get back," but you could tell they did not believe it. Others took defeat calmly, as if admitting that this phase of their life was over. But for the ones I used to call the "rink rats," because they so loved being in the House, their grief at having to say goodbye to the chamber was painful to watch, especially since I felt responsible for their fate. The defeat still felt like an act of nature, a great storm that had knocked down all the trees in the forest. Most caucus colleagues commiserated with me on our common misfortune, while those who felt bitter kept silent. More than one came up and said I had fought a good campaign. There was little recrimination, because I had paid for my mistakes with the loss of my own seat. Zsuzsanna came with me to the last caucus meeting, and when caucus noticed her sitting to one side, weeping with her head in her hands, they rose as one and gave her a standing ovation. She deserved it. No one had worked harder for our common cause. After that, I gave my last speech to caucus, thanked my friends, ignored my enemies and, hand in hand with Zsuzsanna, I strode out of Parliament for the last time.

In the weeks afterward, the solitary reality of defeat began to sink in. It turns out that there is nothing so ex as an ex-politician, especially a defeated one. Your phone goes dead. While I had been in office, ex-politicians refusing to accept their status had occasionally bedevilled my life, and I vowed that having been defeated, I would at least have the good taste not to foist commentary or criticism on my successor, whoever it might be. When you're done in politics, you are well and truly done, and it is a good idea to accept this as quickly as you can. The voters had decided my fate. Now it was my task to accept their verdict and move on.

All this, of course, is easier said than done. As I battled the gloom that came over me, I understood—not immediately, of course, but over time—that the psychic challenge after defeat is to recover your standing. In my case, I had sacrificed my standing as a writer and thinker to enter politics, and now that I had been defeated, I had lost my standing as a politician. Defeat invalidated me as a politician but also as a writer and thinker. I was an embarrassment both to my former political colleagues and to my new ones at the university. I wondered whether I was much use to anybody.

This period of self-pity, I am happy to say, was brief, because defeat had a surprising aspect that I had never anticipated. For five years, I had lived in the public gaze, courting every eye, every glance in the hopes of getting their vote. I had turned myself into a state of complete dependency on the judgment of strangers. Now that they had decided my future, to my immense surprise, strangers came to my rescue. So many e-mails came into party headquarters thanking me for my years in office that the staff bound them in a thick book and presented them to me. Everywhere I went, people came up and congratulated me like someone who'd survived an illness. Keep up the good work, many of them said. Great job, others shouted from the windows of passing cars. I think some of them mistook me for some contestant who had just been voted off a reality TV show, which, in a way, was true.

I'd always assumed that people would praise me on the way up and kick me on the way down, but that's not what defeat was like. Heading out to pick up some dry cleaning a week after the election, back in our condo in Toronto, I passed the firemen lounging in front of the fire station next door, waiting for their next call, and they all gathered around and commiserated on my loss. Tough game, one said, and I said, no tougher than putting out fires. We all laughed. In the dry cleaners opposite our apartment, Michelle, our friend from Vietnam who watches Korean videos on her iPad and never seems to charge us full price for our dry cleaning, came around the counter and gave me a hug. A Sikh truck driver waved brightly as he drove past in his cement mixer. These reactions confirmed me in the view that in politics, the politicians can be awful, the press unspeakable, but the people are actually all right. So many perfect strangers came up to tell me they'd voted for me that you could be forgiven for wondering why we'd lost.

Of course you take defeat personally. You mourn the life you will not get to lead. You mourn the things you will not get to do. I'd finally figured out whom I was doing politics for and now I wouldn't have the chance to do anything for them at all. You grieve and then, as with all forms of grieving that I have gone through, life slowly comes to the rescue. It feels good to have time on your hands, good to be able to read a book again, good to go to a concert. Defeat brings lucidity and it also brings liberation. You get your freedom back when you least expect it. The most surprising reaction to failure is relief.

I began reading again and with reading came the first stirring of the intellectual curiosity, the avidity for ideas that the routine of political life can slowly drive out of your system. Within three weeks of defeat, I started preparing my fall classes, and as I sat in my Massey College office I began thinking about the relation between political life as I had lived it and the great works of political theory that I would once again be teaching.

Naturally enough, I found myself thinking that much of the political theory that students are assigned in classes the world over was written not by those who succeeded in politics but by those who failed. Cicero's *On Duties* and *On Rhetoric*, taught to students of politics for two thousand years, were composed by a man who once wrote a friend, "I used to sit on the deck and hold the rudder of the state in my hands; now there's scarcely room for me in the bilge."[1] The brilliant defender of the Roman republic who held the consul's office was to meet his death at the hands of imperial assassins. As for Machiavelli, another staple of politics classes for five hundred years, he wrote *The Prince* and the *Discourses* only after he had been turfed out of office in 1512, thrown into jail, tortured and sent back to his estates to brood on rejection and defeat. I felt a deep kinship with him now as I read the wonderful letter to his friend Francesco Vettori in which he describes the days of a defeated politician, snaring birds on his estate, chopping wood in the forest, grousing with friends in the tavern and then returning at night to his library, donning the clothes he once wore at court and entering the vanished but consoling world of the Roman classics.[2] Another large figure in the canon of political theory, Edmund Burke, had to live with the criticism that he was never as good a politician as he was a thinker. He wrote *Reflections on the Revolution in France* in 1790, the most penetrating conservative critique of revolutionary ardour, but was ridiculed by the poet Oliver Goldsmith's memorable barb about the politician.[3]

> *Who, born for the Universe, narrow'd his mind,*
> *And to party gave up, what was meant for mankind.*
> *Tho' fraught with all learning, kept straining his throat,*
> *To persuade Tommy Townshend to lend him a vote.*

James Madison co-wrote *The Federalist Papers* with Alexander Hamilton to secure public support for the ratification of the US Constitution. It's still the most successful and vivid political pamphlet in history, but Madison's tenure as president was not exactly crowned with success. He became the only president to flee the White House and endured the sack of his capital city at the hands of the British in the War of 1812. Alexis de Tocqueville, author of the greatest single observation of democracy as a culture of universal aspiration, *Democracy in America*, mouldered on the backbenches of the French parliament throughout the 1840s, writing bitterly about the idiotic speech-making of his fellow MPs. He rose briefly to ministerial office after the revolution of 1848, but in 1851 he retired from politics in disgust.[4] John Stuart Mill may have been the greatest theorist of representative government who ever lived, but as an MP in the British Parliament from 1865 to 1868, he chafed at the legislative incompetence of his fellow MPs and was defeated in his second election.[5] Max Weber, the German sociologist and aristocratic liberal, failed even to gain nomination as a candidate for the Democratic Party in 1919. As an activist, he knew humiliation and defeat. As a theorist, we still assign him to students every year.

Why theoretical acumen is so frequently combined with political failure throws light on what is distinctive about a talent for politics. The candour, rigour, willingness to follow a thought wherever it leads, the penetrating search for originality—all these are virtues in theoretical pursuits but active liabilities in politics, where discretion and dissimulation are essential for success. This would suggest that these theorists failed because they couldn't keep their mouths shut when flattery or partisan discipline required it of them. Equally, however, theorists may have lacked those supreme virtues that separate successful politicians from failures: adaptability, cunning, rapid-fire recognition of Fortuna, the keen intuition that a situation has changed and that what was true once is no longer so, together with the noble capacity to lead, to charm and to inspire.

Thinkers too often disparage men of action in ways that do them no credit. Supreme Court Justice Oliver Wendell Holmes reportedly said of Franklin Roosevelt that he had a second-class intelligence but a first-class temperament. Holmes was being condescending.[6] Roosevelt himself was happy to admit that he had no theory of politics, other than being a Christian and a Democrat, but no theorist could have created the modern liberal state and revived his people's faith in politics in the pit of the Depression. Those with a gift for action, for their part, often express contempt for those whose gifts are more reflective. Men of action like to say, "Those who can, do, those who can't, teach," forgetting that those who teach get to write the history books.

You would think very poorly of me if you supposed that I believe I belong in this company. Neither my actual experience nor my reflections on it put me anywhere near their league. I'm simply taking consolation where I can, and what I learned from them, of course, is that failure in politics has its own authority, not equivalent to the validation of success, but the authority of lived experience. Those who have failed in politics have paid for what they know, and those who pay for knowledge in the real currency of life are entitled to a hearing.

These writers are inspiring in another way. They took a very specific experience—the Roman republic in its final decline, the Florentine republic as it tumbled into dictatorship, the American republic in its fiery birth, French politics in the dog days of Louis Philippe, the British Parliament in its imperial heyday, and the stillbirth of German democracy after 1918—and lifted that specific experience into a generic reflection about the essence of politics. They knew that all politics is local—as we say—shaped by the institutions and historical context that frame the political battle, but they also sought to penetrate to the core of politics as the noblest and most vexatious of all human activities. Thanks to their struggle to locate the generic within the specifics of their own experience, they have given everyone who has ever served in the front lines of politics the vocabulary to comprehend what they have lived through. And for those contemplating a career in politics, these great writers have always offered the debutant the unvarnished reality of the game, if a debutant would only listen.

Several weeks after my defeat, I went to thank Peter Munk, a wealthy man who had given generously to my campaign despite making no bones about voting for my opponents. There aren't many good sports like him left. As partisanship gets worse, ecumenical generosity diminishes. He's the rare exception. Over lunch he told me about a time in the 1970s when a company he started—Clairtone—went bankrupt. After its liquidation, he walked around in the financial district feeling there was a bull's eye on his back. He'd recovered his fortune and much more since then, but he had never forgotten what it was like to fail. In the weeks after my defeat, I had lots of advice from successful people about how to recover. Write romantic fiction, the real estate developer Elvio DelZotto told me, and make yourself some money for a change. David Peterson, who had suffered a bruising defeat as premier of Ontario, told me the good thing about defeat is that you regain the right to tell people to go to hell. Peterson is living proof of the adage "living well is the best revenge," but he added that it took him years to work the pain of failure out of his system. Hard physical exercise helps, he said. Chop down trees, clear brush, build yourself a cabin. Another friend thought he was being comforting when he said at least I'd get a good book out of it. I told him I hadn't gone into politics to get a good book out of it.

The remark I remember best, the one that got me thinking about the book I *did* want to write, came from a taxi driver. As I got into his cab, he pulled his rear-view mirror to get a closer look.

"Are you who I think you are?"

"I am," I said.

"I voted for you."

"I'm glad somebody did."

Then he shrugged and said, "It's politics."

It was if he was saying, "Look, this is how the world is. You did not know it before. You know it now." As we talked, I learned that he was from Lebanon and had been in Canada for twenty years. He combined a cabbie's shrewd grasp of the democratic politics of his new country and a sardonic memory of the brutal confessional politics of Lebanon. I began to see that "politics" was the word he used for the baffling combination of will and chance that determines the shape of life. The way taxi medallions are awarded in a city, for example, was politics. The way dictators continue to rule poor countries was politics, the way Lebanon was carved up by the civil war was politics and, he was saying, the way well-meaning innocents get beaten was politics. When I paid my fare and left him, I wanted more than anything to write about this politics, this brutal game, this dramatic encounter between fate and will, malignity and nobility that fascinated him as much as it fascinated me.

On August 22, barely three months after winning the greatest political victory of his life, Jack Layton died of cancer at his home at the age of sixty-one. Along with thousands of others, Zsuzsanna and I attended his memorial service in Toronto's Roy Thomson Hall and afterward walked home through streets filled with melancholy citizens struggling to come to terms with the bitter ironies of fate. I remember a conversation with one woman who wanted to explain why the media were wrong for criticizing Jack for failing to disclose the true state of his health when he was campaigning. "I'm a cancer survivor," she said. "You say what you have to say. You believe what you have to believe, in order to get through it. Politics doesn't come into it." I could only agree.

Sometime in late August, I went to see the Red Sox play the Blue Jays in the Rogers Centre in Toronto. I love the game. My mother loved it too and we spent happy hours of my childhood watching games on a black-and-white TV. Even the game's *longeurs* are loveable because they offer opportunities for reverie. As the beer cans and hot dog wrappers accumulated at my feet, I got to thinking that what politics most closely resembles is sports. There is the same team play, the same locker room banter and the same pain when you get beaten. Trouble is, we call politics a game, but it isn't one. There is no referee and the teams make up the rules as they go along. You can't cry foul or offside in politics. Almost anything goes. In sports you play by the rules. In politics you just play and the winner re-writes the rules afterwards.

I recalled a wonderful passage in Tolstoy's *War and Peace*, in which Prince Andrei, waiting for the Battle of Borodino, reflects on the difference between war and chess. In chess a bishop is always more powerful than a pawn, while in battle a platoon can sometimes overpower a company.[7] War, in other words, has no rules—just strategies. There is an unpredictable element—will, courage and chance—that can decide outcomes. That also seemed true of politics, a supreme encounter between skill and willpower and the forces of fortune and chance.

Finally, sitting there in the stands as the late afternoon shadows moved across the field, I reflected on the way failure is built into baseball the way it is built into politics. "All political careers eventually end in tears," someone once said. It's also true of sports. All the great careers in sports end in rueful acceptance that muscle memory, killer instinct and inner fire have mysteriously ebbed away. But failure does not just frame the end of every sports career. It's built into the moments of success too. The greatest people who ever played the game of base-ball reached base only three times for every ten they were at the plate. In the late innings of the game, I began to watch the batters after a failed at-bat, how they returned to the dugout, ignored the crowd, never tossed their batting helmet, and withdrew into themselves, mentally adjusting some feature of their action so that they would knock it out of the park next time. There was a discipline at work here with these journeymen baseball players that struck me as admirable. As the game came to an end and the stands began to empty, I thought back to the night I lost the election, standing at a podium in front of a disconsolate crowd that already was dwindling and beginning to file away into the night. I had always been aware, throughout my political career, that down there in the crowd or out there watching on TV, was a young man or woman who would be thinking, *I could be him.* That young person was still out there. I hoped he or she was thinking, *He didn't get there, but I will.* Now I felt, with all my heart, that I wanted to give them every encouragement. *I didn't get there, but you will.*

I realized the truth of what Elinor Caplan, a retired politician, once told me: you're never out of politics. You may have been sent back up into the stands, but you'll still be watching the game. I'm up in the stands now, watching the ones who are stepping forward to take my generation's place, and I'm waiting for the one—the natural—who has what it takes. Everything I've written is for the young man or woman who believed in me and saw me fail. I'm writing this to help them succeed when their time comes. I took a long time to understand whom I was doing politics for. Now I know. I took a long time to understand what politics should be about. Now I know that too, and it is what I want to talk about now, at the very end.

TEN
THE CALLING

YOU MIGHT WELL DRAW the wrong conclusion from this tale of mine. You might be thinking that politics is a dirty game that should be no business of yours. I hope you'll finish reading this book believing something very different: that it's a noble struggle that will require more self-command, judgment and inner toughness than you ever thought you possessed. The nobility lies in the battle to defend what you believe and mobilize others in the fight to preserve what is best about our common life as a people. The challenge lies in trying to change what must be changed and preserving what must be preserved, and knowing the difference between the two.

Before you enter the political arena, old hands may tell you to be careful, not to say or do anything that will tarnish your chances in the future. You will be told not to accumulate baggage. I entered politics with a lot of baggage and I paid full freight for it, but it's better to have paid up than to have lived a defensive life. A defensive life is not a life fully lived. If you take prudence as your watchword, your courage will desert you when the time comes to show your mettle. You can be sure that politics will demand more of you than prudence.

You can't know, in advance, what you're in for, but really, our lack of foresight in life is a blessing. Don't be afraid to take the plunge and don't be afraid to fail. If you can free yourself of the idea that failure is a disgrace, you won't be crushed by it and you won't be spoiled by success either. Strive for success and don't allow any excuses for failure, but above all learn equanimity. You can always control the factors that depend on you alone—your courage, will, determination and humour— but you can't control the forces that come into play when you enter the public arena. Since Fortuna largely determines political careers, you have no reason to rail at fate if she turns against you. Don't make the mistake of supposing you control your fate. That's called hubris.

Embracing a political life means shedding your innocence. It means being willing to pay the costs before you even know what they are going to be. It means knowing who you are and being adamant about what a political life is for. You can't succeed unless the people who elect you believe that you're in it for them. If you're not in it for them, you shouldn't be in politics. It might take a long time to figure out who you do politics for. You learn this slowly over a hundred meetings with strangers and you gradually take their cause to be your own. They become the people you serve and the ones you justify yourself to. Becoming their representative is a relationship that changes you for- ever, and its rewards are great. If they believe in you, they will stick with you through thick and thin.

You aren't entitled to their loyalty. You earn it from them every day. You earn it by being who you say you are and by showing that you are on their side. If you have standing with them, they will stick with you even when they disagree. They will trust you to lead them if they believe your convictions are sincere.

Citizens know the difference between someone who seeks their approval and someone who seeks their respect. You don't always have to be popular to succeed. Your people don't have to like you but they must respect you, feel that you have integrity, believe that you are working for them.

Your opponents will try to define you, and if they succeed they will have beaten you, so you must keep control of your story. The story you need to tell should be about the community and country you want to build. You need to tell a story that links your fate to theirs, your life to theirs, your cause to their own. You need to fit policy and your personal story into a convincing narrative. The story you need to tell is how to strengthen the common life, how to stand together against the forces of inequality, envy, division and hatred that are ceaselessly pulling our societies apart, and how to defend the eternal proposition of all progressive politics: that we must share our fate and live in justice with each other. A story about shared fate and justice will be a national story, one that should draw upon all the sources of common experience that hold us together as citizens and give us common allegiance to one another and to our institutions. It will be a story that tells us we should be better than we are.

Antagonism is the essence of politics and you will need a fighter's temperament in order to prevail. People won't stand with someone who doesn't know how to defend himself. Of course it's painful to be attacked, but really it's a kind of vanity to take it personally. Becoming an adult is a matter of learning never to take things personally: defend your honour and integrity, by all means, but never allow your inner core to be touched by personal attack. Do not give your opponents the satisfaction. At all times defend your standing, your right to be heard.

You will give as good as you get in combat, but a wise politician knows the difference between a clean hit and a dirty one. Voters may vote for politicians who fight dirty, but they don't like them, and you're in politics to earn respect, not fear.

You don't want to be an innocent, but you don't want to be a cynic either. You don't want to succumb to the cynicism that says voters don't know what they want and don't care. You need to keep faith in the judgment of the people, no matter how often their votes go against you, no matter how often your faith in them may be tried. If you don't believe in the ultimate rationality of citizens, you don't have the faith needed to make democracy work. Democracy only deserves its moral privilege if there are good reasons to believe in the judgment of the people. Accepting their verdict can be hard at times, but there is no other referee.

To enjoy politics and to do it well, you have to believe that you serve everyone, whether they voted for you or not. Even when political reality forces you to choose one group's interests over another's, you should never forget that the losers have paid a price for the choices you've made. To be a good politician is to be responsible *to* the people who put you there, and to be responsible *for* your actions.

This faith in the people is on trial in our time. In fully half the world there are regimes that combine authoritarian oligarchy with market principles—China and Russia come to mind. They all proclaim their superiority to the cumbersome, partisan, divided democratic politics of our free societies. We have no reason to suppose that democracy's eventual victory in this battle of ideas is assured. There is no guarantee that history is on liberty's side or that democracy will prevail against its resurgent competitors. Seen in this international dimension, a politician's duty is not just to defend democracy at home but to vindicate its virtues to the larger world. You are in the arena because the vindication democracy needs most is not in words but in deeds, not in theory but in action.

You are the custodian of democracy, of a relationship of trust with the people, but also of the institutions of your country. If you get to serve in a legislature, try not to forget the wonder you felt on your first day, when you took your seat and you understood that it was the votes of ordinary people who put you there. Try to remember, too, that you are not smarter than your institutions. They are there to make you better than you are. Respect for traditions, for the rules, even some of the silly ones, is part of your respect for the sovereignty of the people and for the democracy that keeps us free. Respect for institutions means you shoulder an obligation to treat your adversaries as opponents, never as enemies. Politics is not war: it is our only reliable alternative to it. Democracy cannot function without a culture of respect for your antagonist. In politics, you have loyalties to yourself, to your party, to the people who voted for you, but also to the country. Since these loyalties conflict, you will want to be clear before you start that there may come a time when you have to put your country first.

In keeping your loyalties straight, it pays to have an appropriate respect for politics itself. We talk about politics as if it were just a game, but it's too serious for that. We are legislators after all, and there may come a time when you will have to vote to send young men and women to fight and die. It's not a game when the consequences are as large as these.

Politics is not "show business for ugly people." The politicians I worked with weren't in it for low-wattage celebrity. They wanted to serve someone, somehow, and most judged how well they were doing by whether they had achieved anything for their constituents. That's the metric that matters, the one that keeps you honest.

Politics isn't a profession either, since a profession implies standards and techniques that can be taught. There are no techniques in politics: it is not a science but a charismatic art, dependent on skills of persuasion, oratory and bloody-minded perseverance, all of which can be learned in life but none of which can be taught in a classroom or a consultant's office. It's also not a profession in the sense of a steady career. Your life in politics can be upended in an instant, so you need to make sure you had a life before and can be prepared to resume a new life afterwards. Knowing that you can stand to lose is the best guarantee that you can stay honest.

In a lecture he gave to frightened students in revolutionary Munich in January 1919, as they tried to get their bearings amidst the street violence that followed Germany's defeat in World War I, Max Weber distinguished those who lived *off* politics from those who lived *for* politics. Only those who live for politics can understand it as a calling. His final words to those students are worth repeating here:

> Politics is a strong and slow boring of hard boards. It takes both passion and perspective. Certainly all historical experience confirms the truth—that man would have not attained the possible unless time and again he had reached out for the impossible. But to do that a man must be a leader, and not only a leader but a hero as well, in a very sober sense of the word. And even those who are neither leaders or heroes must arm themselves with that steadfastness of heart which can brave even the crumbling of all hopes. This is necessary right now, or else men will not be able to attain even that which is possible today. Only he has the calling for politics who is sure that he shall not crumble when the world from his point of view is too stupid or too base for what he wants to offer. Only he who in the face of all this can say, "In spite of all" has the calling for politics.[1]

I would counsel you to think of politics as a calling. The term is usually reserved for priests, nuns and mystics, but there is something appealing about using it for work as sinful and worldly as politics. It captures precisely what is so hard: to be worldly and sinful and yet faithful and fearless at the same time. You put your own immodest ambitions in the service of others. You hope that your ambitions will be redeemed by the good you do. In the process you get your hands dirty for the sake of ends that are supposed to be clean. You use human vices—cunning and ruthlessness—in the service of the virtues—justice and decency. You serve the only divinity left—the people—and you have to learn to submit to their verdicts. These verdicts can be painful and hard to understand, but we have nothing else in which we can put our faith, insofar as our common life is concerned.

Cynics will dismiss this vision of politics as a piece of self-important delusion, but for those who have actually done it, like me, it has a ring of truth. It is a vision of what politics could be that enables you to understand what politics actually is. It is in the nature of a calling that it remains beyond our grasp. Those who are called know they are not worthy of it, but it inspires them all the same. So think of politics as a calling that inspires us onward, ever onward, like a guiding star. Those of us who answered the call know that success or failure matters less to us than the simple fact that we did answer it. What we hope now is that others, more resolute, more daring, more devoted, will answer it too. It is for these young men and women that this book was written.

NOTES

CHAPTER ONE

1. Mario Vargas Llosa, *A Fish in the Water*, transl. Helen Lane Farrar (New York: FSG, 1994); Václav Havel, *To the Castle and Back*, transl. Paul Wilson (New York: Knopf, 2007); Carlos Fuentes, *Myself with Others* (New York,: FSG, 1988).

CHAPTER TWO

1. See my *The Russian Album* (London: Vintage, 1987).
2. George Ignatieff, *The Making of a Peacemonger* (Toronto: University of Toronto Press, 1985), p. 73.
3. George Monro Grant, *Ocean to Ocean* (Toronto, 1873); see also my *True Patriot Love* (Toronto: Penguin, 2009).
4. W. L. Grant, *Principal Grant* (Toronto, 1903).
5. George H. Ford, ed., *The Pickersgill Letters, 1934–1943* (Toronto: Ryerson Press, 1948); Jonathan Vance, *Unlikely Soldiers: How Two Canadians Fought the Secret War Against Nazi Occupation* (Toronto: HarperCollins, 2008).
6. Victor Gruen, *The Heart of Our Cities: The Urban Crisis: Diagnosis and Cure* (London: Thames and Hudson, 1965).
7. http://www.youtube.com/watch?v=_E3-_z5YP0M.
8. Pierre Trudeau, *Memoirs* (Toronto: McClelland and Stewart, 1993). See the illustrations, p. 369.

9. See my *The Rights Revolution: The Massey Lectures* (Toronto: Anansi, 1999).

10. See my "Liberal Values in the 21st Century," address to the Biennial Policy Conference, Liberal Party of Canada, Ottawa, March 3, 2005.

CHAPTER THREE

1. Niccolo Machiavelli, *The Prince* (1513), ed. and transl. David Wootton (New York: Hackett, 1994), ch. 25.

2. There is some dispute as to whether Macmillan actually made his famous remark. Elizabeth M. Knowles, ed., *What They Didn't Say: A Book of Misquotations* (Oxford: Oxford University Press, 2006), pp. vi, 33.

3. See my *The Lesser Evil* (Princeton: Princeton University Press, 2004).

4. See my *Blood and Belonging* (Toronto: Penguin, 1993), p. 123.

5. Ibid., p. 146.

6. "… torture should remain anathema to a liberal democracy and should never be regulated, countenanced or covertly accepted in a war on terror. For torture, when committed by a state, expresses the state's ultimate view that human beings are expendable. This view is antithetical to the spirit of any constitutional society whose raison d'etre is the control of violence and coercion in the name of human dignity and freedom." Ignatieff, *The Lesser Evil*, p. 143.

7. Ignatieff, *The Russian Album* (London: Penguin, 1997 ed.), epilogue.

8. Ernest Renan, "What is a Nation?" http://www.nationalismproject.org/what/renan.htm.

9. http://www.theatlanticwire.com/politics/2013/02/ed-koch-obituaries/61684/.

10. http://www.poetrymagnumopus.com/index.php?showtopic=1685. The translation has been altered by Zsuzsanna Zsohar.

CHAPTER FOUR

1. Baldesar Castiglione, *The Book of the Courtier* (London: Penguin Classics, 1967), p. 67.

2. Ignatieff, *Blood and Belonging*, p. 212.

3. The Conservative motion read: "That this House recognize that the Québécois form a nation within a united Canada." November 27, 2006.

4. Benedict Anderson, *Imagined Communities: Reflections on the Origins and Spread of Nationalism* (New York: Verso, 1991).

CHAPTER FIVE

1. http://www.elections.ca/content.aspx?section=fin&dir=lea&document=index&lang=e; http://www.elections.ca/content.aspx?section=vot&dir=faq&document=faqelec&lang=e#a15; http://www.fec.gov/press/press2009/20090608PresStat.shtml; http://www.opensecrets.org/news/2012/10/2012-election-spending-will-reach-6.html.

2. This is how the law stood in 2006. Since 2011, the Harper government has phased out per-vote subsidies for political parties and reduced donation limits.

3. United States Supreme Court "Citizens United v. Federal Election Commission," 2010, http://www.supremecourt.gov/opinions/09pdf/08-205.pdf.

4. www.nytimes.com/2009/08/11/opinion/11tue4.html.

5. See my *Isaiah Berlin: A Life* (London: Chatto, 1998).

6. See my "Canada and Israel: A Personal Perspective on the Ties That Bind," an address to Holy Blossom Synagogue, Toronto, April 13, 2008.

CHAPTER SIX

1. Doris Kearns Goodwin, *Team of Rivals: The Political Genius of Abraham Lincoln* (New York: Simon and Schuster, 2005).

2. www.chu.cam.ac.uk/archives/exhibitions/Ottawa_image.php.

3. http://www.hillwatch.com/pprc/quotes/parliament_and_cabinet.aspx.

4. Amy Gutmann and Dennis Thompson, *Democracy and Disagreement* (Cambridge: Harvard University Press, 1996).

5. Jane Mansbridge, "A Selection Model of Representation," Kennedy School of Government research paper, 2008. See also Hanna Pitkin, *The Concept of Representation* (Berkeley: University of California, 1967).

6. https://www.gov.uk/government/publications/the-coalition-documentation. See also P. H. Russell, *Two Cheers for Minority Government* (Toronto: Montgomery, 2008).

CHAPTER SEVEN

1. http://www.youtube.com/watch?v=eVJ3eSN6MBM.

2. http://www.youtube.com/watch?v=ngjUkPbGwAg. See also Drew Westen, *The Political Brain: The Role of Emotion in Deciding the Fate of the Nation* (New York: Public Affairs, 2012), ch. 2.

3. Barack Obama, "Towards a More Perfect Union" speech, Philadelphia Constitution Hall, March 2008, http://www.youtube.com/watch?v=zrp-v2tHaDo.

4. The key US decisions on standing are Frothingham v. Mellon, 262 U.S. 447 (1923); Fairchild v. Hughes, 258 U.S. 126 (1922); Bond v. United States, 529 U.S. 334 (2000); Allen v. Wright, 468 U.S. at 757 (1984); and Lujan v. Defenders of Wildlife, 504 U.S. at 562 (1992). I am grateful to Brent Kettles and Mike Pal for helpful comments and suggestions on standing, US election law and the comparison with Canadian law in these areas. A key Canadian decision on standing is Canadian Council of Churches v. Canada (Minister of Employment and Immigration), [1992] 1 S.C.R. 236.

5. Sasha Issenberg, *The Victory Lab* (New York: Crown, 2012); Thomas Byrne Edsall, *The Age of Austerity: How Scarcity Will Remake American Politics* (New York: Doubleday, 2012).

6. For a contrary view see Russell Hardin, *How Do You Know? The Economics of Ordinary Knowledge* (Princeton: Princeton University Press, 2009).

7. I argue this further in "Rationality in Politics," the Edna Ullmann Margalit Lecture at the Center for the Study of Rationality, Hebrew University of Jerusalem, January 4, 2013. In particular I want to thank Avishai Margalit and Moshe Halbertal for their comments.

8. Drew Westen, *The Political Brain* (New York: Public Affairs, 2008); George Lakoff, *The Political Mind* (New York: Viking, 2008). See also Daniel Kahneman, *Thinking Fast and Slow* (New York: Doubleday, 2012).

9. Abraham Lincoln, First Inaugural Address, March 4, 1861, http://www.nationalcenter.org/LincolnFirstInaugural.html.

CHAPTER EIGHT

1. http://www.liberal.ca/newsroom/news-release/speakers-announced-for-canada-at-150-rising-to-the-challenge/.

2. http://www.scribd.com/doc/50397233/Speaker-s-ruling-BRISON-Privilege-Production-of-Document. One Canadian foundation—Samara—has made the state of democratic governance in Canada a central theme. See http://www.samaracanada.com.

3. Nancy Rosenblum, *On the Side of the Angels: An Appreciation of Parties and Partisanship* (Princeton: Princeton University Press, 2008).

4. Max Weber, "Politics as a Vocation," in H. H. Gerth and C. W. Mills, eds., *From Max Weber* (New York: Oxford University Press, 1958), pp. 77–128.

5. Jimmie Maxton, quoted in Bernard Crick, *In Defence of Politics* (London: Weidenfeld and Nicolson, 1992), p. 138.

6. Carl von Clausewitz, *On War*, ed. Michael Howard and Peter Paret (Princeton: Princeton University Press, 1976).

7. Amy Gutmann and Dennis Thompson, *The Spirit of Compromise: Why Governing Demands It and Campaigning Undermines It* (Princeton:

Princeton University Press, 2012); Arthur Isak Applbaum, *Ethics for Adversaries: The Morality of Roles in Public and Professional Life* (Princeton: Princeton University Press, 1999).

8. Avishai Margalit, *On Compromise and Rotten Compromises* (Princeton: Princeton University Press, 2009).

CHAPTER NINE

1. Marcus Tullius Cicero, *How to Run a Country: An Ancient Guide for Modern Leaders*, ed. and intro. by Philip Freeman (Princeton: Princeton Univeristy Press, 2012), p. xi.

2. Niccolo Machiavelli, *Selected Political Writings*, ed. and transl. David Wootton (Cambridge: Hackett, 1994), pp. 1–4.

3. Edmund Burke, *Stanford Encyclopedia of Philosophy*, http://plato. stanford.edu/entries/burke/.

4. Alexis de Tocqueville, *Lettres choisies, Souvenirs, 1814–1859* (Paris: Gallimard, 2003).

5. John Stuart Mill, "Considerations on Representative Government," ch. V. in J. S. Mill, *On Liberty and Other Essays*, ed. John Gray (Oxford: Oxford University Press, 1991).

6. See Louis Menand, "How the Deal Went Down," *New Yorker*, March 4, 2013. See also Isaiah Berlin, "President Franklin Delano Roosevelt," in *The Proper Study of Mankind: An Anthology of Essays*, ed. Henry Hardy and Roger Hausheer (London: Chatto and Windus, 1997), pp. 628–37.

7. Leo Tolstoy, *War and Peace*, transl. Richard Pevear and Larissa Volokhonsky (New York: Vintage, 2007), Book 10, ch. XXV:

    "And yet they say that war is like a game of chess?" he remarked.

    "Yes," replied Prince Andrew, "but with this little difference, that in chess you may think over each move as long as you please and are not limited for time, and with this difference too, that a knight is always stronger than a pawn, and two pawns are always stronger than one, while in war a battalion is sometimes stronger than a division and sometimes weaker than a company. The relative strength of bodies of troops can never be known to anyone. Believe me," he went on, "if things depended on arrangements made by the staff, I should be there making arrangements, but instead of that I have the honor to serve here in the regiment with these gentlemen, and I consider that on us tomorrow's battle will depend and not on those others. . . . Success never depends, and never will depend, on position, or equipment, or even on numbers, and least of all on position."

"But on what then?"

"On the feeling that is in me and in him," he pointed to Timokhin, "and in each soldier."

CHAPTER TEN

1. Max Weber, "Politik als Beruf" ["Politics as a Vocation"], in H. H. Gerth and C. W. Mills, eds., *From Max Weber,* (New York: Oxford University Press, 1958), p. 128. See also Max Weber, *Political Writings,* ed. Peter Lassman and Ronald Speirs (Cambridge: Cambridge University Press, 1994); Fritz Ringer, *Max Weber: An Intellectual Biography* (Chicago: University of Chicago Press, 2004); Terry Maley, *Democracy and the Political in Max Weber's Thought* (Toronto: University of Toronto Press, 2011).

INDEX

Note: "MI" references denote Michael Ignatieff.

aboriginal peoples
  and politics, 146
  on reserves, 65, 74
  residential school apology, 145–46
adversaries
  as allies, 152
  as enemies, 150–52
  as opponents, 181
advertising. *See* attack ads
Afghanistan
  detainee transfers, 98, 144
  troop commitments, 99
"An Agenda for Nation Building"
  (Ignatieff), 72–74
Aggarwal, Sachin, 28, 41
Alexandar, Georges, 154
ambition, 7–10, 13
Apps, Alfred ("the men in
  black"), 1–2, 24, 25, 38, 47

Arab-Israeli wars, 15–16
asbestos exports, 149
attack ads, 132, 133
  against Dion, 99–100, 106
  in 2011 election, 157, 158–59
  against MI, 120–24, 157
  MI's response, 123–26
  as permanent campaign, 71, 133
  truth in, 122, 123
  in United States, 121–22
  and voters, 129, 132
Attila, József ("By the Danube"),
  45–46
Augustine, Jean, 35, 36, 38, 41
automobile industry, 118

bad faith, 38, 79
Bagnell, Larry, 149
baseball, 174–75

Berlin, Isaiah, 77

Blair, Tony, 30

Bloc Québécois, 60, 63, 160. *See also* Duceppe, Gilles
and coalition crisis, 108–9
in Parliament, 96–97
as rival party, 110

Blood and Belonging (Ignatieff), 36

Book of the Courtier (Castiglione), 57–58

Brison, Scott, 158–59

Brock, Dan ("the men in black"), 1–2, 24, 25, 38, 47

Brown, Gordon, 24, 30

bureaucracy, 17, 104–6

Burke, Edmund, 169

Bush, George W., 122
MI as apologist for, 35, 37, 52

"By the Danube" (Attila), 45–46

Canada. *See also* elections; Parliament
constitution, 62
divisions in, 63–65, 73
federal-provincial relations, 74
as "imagined community," 64
MI and, 27–28, 63–64
monarchy's role, 93
national unity, 61–63
as political entity, 27, 64

recession in, 106–7, 112, 117, 119, 138, 139
in Second World War, 11

Canadian Broadcasting Corporation, 27

Canadian Foreign Service, 15

candour, 7, 80

canvassing, 38–40, 42–43, 44

Caplan, Elinor, 175

carbon tax, 107

Casteura, Expie, 116

Castiglione, Baldassare, 57–58

Chalifoux, Marc, 53, 86

Chalk River Nuclear Laboratories, 17, 99

Chan, Milton, 28, 41

China, 180

Choudhry, Sujit, 28

Chrétien, Jean, 24, 42, 60, 116

Churchill, Winston, 94

Cicero, Marcus Tullius, 169

citizenship
as binding force, 64, 73, 124
as freedom, 73

Citizenship and Immigration, 105

civil servants, 17, 104–6

Clausewitz, Carl von, 151

Clinton, Bill, 57, 127

coalition crisis (2008), 108–12, 116, 117–18

MI's position, 109–10, 116–17, 147

communities

countries as, 64, 95

distinctiveness of, 61–65

as political blocs, 82

reaction to attack, 77–78

Conant, Armand, 38

conscription debate (1944), 116

Conservative Party of Canada,
73, 152. *See also* Harper,
Stephen

in 2006 election, 46

in 2011 election, 157, 161

in Etobicoke–Lakeshore, 40, 44

during Liberal leadership
campaign, 62–63

in opposition, 25

corruption, 44, 60, 72

cosmopolitanism, 27, 124

Cotler, Irwin, 110

"data monkeys," 41, 44, 119

Daughters of the Empire, 17

Davey, Ian, 45, 69, 76, 137

as "man in black," 1–2, 24, 25,
38, 47

Davey, Keith, 1

Davis, Brad, 41

defence issues, 99, 143

DelZotto, Elvio, 28, 172

democracy

civility in, 151

connection to place, 54–55

as daily plebiscite, 39–40

entitlement in, 13

Harper's contempt for, 102–3,
145

House of Commons and,
95–98

Internet and, 55

opposition's role, 150–51

persuasion in, 95–96, 150–51

public involvement in, 102–3,
151, 180

and standing, 133–34

worldwide, 180

Democracy in America
(Tocqueville), 170

Dion, Stéphane

attack ads against, 99–100, 106

in leadership race, 51, 86

MI and, 91, 110

as party leader, 90, 108–10, 111

Discourses (Machiavelli), 169

dissimulation, 17, 144, 170

diversity, 41–42

Donolo, Peter, 160

Dosanjh, Ujjal, 144

Dow Chemical, 19

Drache, Josh, 116

Dryden, Ken, 51, 72

Duceppe, Gilles, 96–97, 108, 137, 160. *See also* Bloc Québécois

Duplessis, Maurice, 19

On Duties and *On Rhetoric* (Cicero), 169

education, 73
  as entitlement, 127, 157

Eisenhower, Dwight D., 16

Eizenga, Mike, 28, 38

elections, 128–29
  in 1960s, 19, 20
  in 2004, 24
  in 2006, 33, 38–46
  in 2008, 106–7
  in 2011, 153–61
  canvassing in, 38–40, 42–43, 44
  fixed dates for, 106
  funding for, 70–72
  rallies, 154–56
  television debates, 160

Elections Canada, 70–71

Elizabeth II, Her Majesty the Queen, 93

employment insurance, 138

endorsements, 52, 128, 129

energy policies, 74

entitlement, 13, 53, 129, 133, 178
  education as, 127, 157

environmental issues, 90, 107

equality of opportunity, 83–84, 140, 153

Esterhazy (SK), 59

Etobicoke–Lakeshore riding
  campaigns in, 38–45, 107
  canvassing in, 38–40, 42–43, 44
  as Member of Parliament for, 91, 103–6
  nomination as candidate, 35–38
  office and staff, 38–39, 40–41
  opposition in, 36–38, 40, 44–45
  supporters in, 38, 41–42, 84–85

expatriates, 27, 123–24

expediency *vs.* principle, 148–50

External Affairs, Department of, 15

failure, 172, 177–78
  importance of, 23, 171
  life after, 168–71
  in sports, 174–75

The Federalist Papers (Madison and Hamilton), 170

financial crisis. *See* recession

Fleming, Sandford, 12

Fortuna, 33–34, 46, 87, 159, 171, 178

Fowler, Robert, 139

Fraser, Graham, 29

Fraser, John, 165

freedom, 73

Frost, Robert, 18

F-35 fighters, 143

Fuentes, Carlos, 2

fundraising, 70–72, 92–93

Gagnon, Lysiane, 156

Garneau, Marc, 143

Gelber, Marvin, 19

Gendron, Marc, 86

Geneva Conventions

   and Afghan detainee transfers,
      144

   Israel Defense Forces and, 76

Globe and Mail, 18

Goldsmith, Oliver, 169

good faith, 38, 79

Goodwin, Doris Kearns, 90

government. *See also* bureau-
      cracy; Parliament

   in austerity, 139–40

   citizens and, 106

   debate within, 151

   and economy, 138, 139–40

   opposition's role, 150–51

   prime minister's role, 8, 74

   regulation of politics by, 71–72

   as unifying force, 16–17

Grant, George Monro "Geordie,"
      12, 13

Grant family, 12–13

Gruen, Victor, 20

G20 summit, Toronto, 143–44

gun control, 43, 63–64, 149

Hamilton, Alexander, 170

Harper, Stephen. *See also* Harper
      government

   and coalition crisis, 119

   combativeness, 98, 99–100, 108,
      143

   contempt for democracy,
      102–3, 145

   in 2006 election, 44

   in 2011 election, 160

   and Israel, 78

   and media, 156–57

   and MI, 100, 117, 119–20

   missteps, 107, 108

   as opportunist, 62–63, 100, 106

   partisan approach, 98–100, 108,
      119, 143

   as party leader, 25, 100

   political skill, 62–63, 100, 106, 138

   and Quebec, 63

   and recession, 107, 108, 119, 138

   and residential school apology,
      145–46

Harper government

   budgets, 117, 138, 153

contempt citations, 144–45, 153

"Dumpster bills," 102

information withheld by,
   143–44

   Liberals and, 137, 143

   as partisan, 104–5, 144, 145

   permanent campaign tactics,
      71, 99–100, 133

   service cuts, 106

   tough-on-crime approach, 98

   wasteful spending, 143–44

Havel, Václav, 2

health care, 73

Hezbollah, 75–76

Holland, Mark, 143

Holmes, Oliver Wendell, 171

House of Commons, 93–95. *See
   also* Harper government;
   Parliament

   democracy at work in, 95–98

   party discipline in, 96, 151

   public alienation from, 100,
      101, 102–3

   Question Period, 97–98, 101

   rancid atmosphere in, 100, 145

Human Rights Watch, 76

Hussein, Saddam, 37

Ignatieff, Alison (née Grant), 10,
   12, 13–15, 23

Ignatieff, Andrew, 24

Ignatieff, George, 10–12, 56

   career, 11, 15, 16, 18–19, 22–23

   Trudeau and, 22–23

Ignatieff, Michael, 2. *See also*
      Ignatieff, Michael: political
      life

   as Canadian, 26–27, 35–38

   childhood and youth, 15, 18

   family roots, 56, 60–61, 125

   French language ability, 59–60

   role models, 15–16

   in United States, 1, 2, 23–24, 26,
      27

Ignatieff, Michael: political life,
      17–18, 40. *See also* Etobicoke–
      Lakeshore riding

   contact with people in, 124–26,
      141–42

   as deputy Liberal leader,
      91–92, 109

   2011 election campaign, 153–60

   end of, 165–67

   as interim Liberal leader,
      111–12, 115–16, 118–19

   liabilities, 25–26

   as Member of Parliament, 89,
      91, 93

   misconceptions about, 35–38,
      52, 123, 159

mistakes, 9, 37, 74–76, 78–79, 137–38

misunderstandings of, 74–79

non-confidence motion, 137

office and staff, 116, 119, 125, 137–38

preparation for, 27–30

support for, 167–68

Ignatieff, Natalie, 10

Ignatieff, Paul, 10

Ignatieff family, 10, 26, 37

immigrants, 16, 63, 105, 173. *See also specific cultural groups*

Internet, 55, 141

damaging material on, 36, 77

Iraq invasion, 35, 37

Israel, 76, 77, 78

Jefferson, Thomas, 72

Jewish community, 75, 76, 78

Johnson, Lyndon B., 21

Kahneman, Daniel, 131

Kancer, Mary, 38, 103

Karsh, Yousuf, 94

Kehoe, Jeff, 53

Kennedy, Gerard, 144

Kennedy, John F., 18

Kennedy, Robert F., 21–22

Kennedy School of Government (Harvard University), 1, 25, 35, 86–87, 90–91

Kerry, John, 121–22

Khalifa, Major, 41

King, Martin Luther, 21, 133

King, William Lyon Mackenzie, 17–18, 116

knowledge

of country, 54–56, 66

political, 28

of self, 9

Koch, Ed, 39

Lalonde, Marc, 30

La Presse, 156

Laurier, Wilfrid, 60, 115

Layton, Jack, 44, 137, 159–60, 173–74. *See also* New Democratic Party

and coalition crisis, 108, 111

Lebanon, 74–75, 173

LeBlanc, Dominic, 108, 111, 143

The Lesser Evil (Ignatieff), 35, 37

Lewis, David, 19

"Liberal Express," 124–26

liberalism, 16–17, 28–29, 157

Liberal Party of Canada. *See also* Liberal Party of Canada: leadership campaigns accomplishments, 17, 43–44, 138

caucus meetings, 95, 126, 142–43, 166

in disarray, 1, 42, 56, 128, 139

in 2011 election, 153–61

as "natural governing party," 25, 46–47

in 1960s, 19, 86

in opposition, 46–47, 56–57, 142–44

as party of the middle, 40

policy conventions, 28–29, 139

and Quebec, 60, 160–61

and recession, 107, 138–40

scandals, 44, 60

support for, 24–25, 43–45, 118, 128, 129

weaknesses, 44–45, 128, 129

Liberal Party of Canada: leadership campaigns, 8, 46–47, 51–81, 108

campaign team, 52, 69–70, 81, 91

challenges, 51, 69

conventions, 47, 51, 81–86

delegates, 51, 82

funding for, 70–72, 92–93

MI as candidate, 52, 56–57, 71, 72–74, 82–85, 90

rival candidates, 51–52, 58–59, 69, 79, 81–82

travels during, 53, 55–56, 59–61

Lincoln, Abraham, 90, 133

loyalty, 178, 181

to constituents, 101–2, 178

to party, 96, 148–49, 151, 152

Macalister, John, 13

Macdonald, John A., 12–13

Machiavelli, Niccolo, 33–35, 169

Macmillan, Harold, 34

Madison, James, 72, 170

Maloney, Jamie, 38

Maloney, Marion, 38

Martin, Paul, 1, 24, 29–30, 42, 46

Massey, Vincent, 11–12, 23

Massey Lectures, 27

Mazer, Alex, 28

McCarthy, Eugene, 21

media, 79–80, 100–101, 124, 140–41. *See also specific media*

and Harper, 156–57

and leadership campaign, 52, 76

Meganetty, Steve, 42

Mercer, Rick, 115

Middle East, 74–76, 79

Mill, John Stuart, 170

Milliken, Peter, 144

Montreal, 75–76, 92

Moore, Kay (Gimpel), 13, 14

Munk, Peter, 172

"My City of Ruins"
    (Springsteen), 155

natural resources, 65

Naylor, David, 165

negative advertising. *See* attack ads

New Democratic Party, 73, 79,
    99, 142. *See also* Layton, Jack
    in Quebec, 159, 161
    as rival party, 40, 107, 110

Nixon, Richard, 127

Obama, Barack, 25, 89, 128–29
    2008 election campaign, 122,
        132–33
    and MI, 57, 117–18

Ocean to Ocean (Grant), 12

Oliphant, Rob, 40–41

opinion polls, 129

"oppo research," 36, 77

opportunism, 34, 62–63, 100, 106,
    112

opportunity (equality of), 83–84,
    140, 153

Pal, Michael, 28

Parkin, Alice, 12

Parkin, George, 12

Parliament, 93–95. *See also*
    House of Commons
    coalition crisis (2008), 108–12
    co-operation in, 99
    Harper's contempt for, 102–3,
        145
    members of, 93, 97–98, 103–6
    prorogation of, 102–3, 111
    public view of, 145, 150

Parliament Buildings, 93–95, 142

partisanship
    of Harper, 98–100, 108, 119, 143
    of Harper government, 104–5,
        144, 145
    in politics, 147–48, 150

Pearson, Lester B. "Mike," 11–12,
    15–16, 19

persuasion, 95–96, 150–51

Peterson, David, 28, 172

Petit, Jerry, 116

Pickersgill, Frank, 13–15

Pickersgill, Jack, 15, 16

Pimblett, Jim, 29

political parties, 41, 91–92. *See
    also* politicians; politics;
    specific parties
    endorsement by, 128
    loyalty to, 148–49, 152
    in opposition, 92, 140–41
    party discipline in, 96, 151

in power, 98

rivalry in, 90, 91

politicians. *See also* political
  parties; politics; standing

vs. civil servants, 17, 104–6

connection with constituents,
  56, 57–58, 59, 131–32, 141–42

definition by opponents, 52,
  179 (*see also* attack ads)

inspiring examples, 21–22

and international issues, 76

knowledge of country, 54–56,
  66

loyalty to constituents, 101–2,
  178

motivation, 7–9, 43

and national institutions,
  180–81

need for grace, 57–58

need for "presence," 101–2

outsiders as, 89

positioning by, 75–76

as public figures, 53, 80–81,
  101–2, 141

self-defence by, 179

separation from constituents,
  101–2, 111–12, 146–47, 152

and spontaneity, 80, 81

story control by, 26, 179

unscrupulous, 23

politics. *See also* liberalism;
  political parties; politicians

adversaries in, 150–52, 181

amateurs in, 69–70, 89

artifice in, 58

as calling, 3–4, 8, 148, 181–83

as combat, 79, 86, 101, 120–21,
  126, 151–52, 179

compromises necessary, 80–81,
  149–50, 152

corruption in, 44, 60, 72

defeat in, 131, 167–71

differentiation in, 138, 147

fascination with, 72, 173

of fear, 157

financial influences, 71–72

as game of words, 76–77, 79–80

government regulation in,
  71–72

ideas in, 74

illusion in, 47

as local, 54–55, 59, 64, 124–25

as loss of innocence, 177–78

negative, 133–34 (*see also* attack
  ads)

partisanship in, 147–48, 150

of permanent campaign,
  99–100, 120–21, 158

as physical, 57

as profession, 89, 181

public alienation from, 101, 145, 148, 150, 151, 183
of resentment, 157
respect in, 180–81
in 1950s and 1960s, 16–17, 18–21
as self-dramatization, 26
as service, 7–8, 181
skills needed, 57–58, 170–71
vs. sports, 174–75
standing in, 126–27
as theory, 168–70, 171–72
timing in, 34
truth in, 8, 61–62
voters' interest in, 42–43, 145
war *vs.*, 174, 181
"Politics as a Vocation" (Weber), 148
pornography, 17
Power, Samantha, 25
Prichard, Rob, 165
The Prince (Machiavelli), 33, 169
principle *vs.* expediency, 148–50
prisons, 98
protests
    against MI, 35–38, 52
    against Vietnam War, 19, 21
prudence, 177

Quebec, 22, 59–63, 159, 160–61

Rae, Bob, 30, 51–52, 144
    and coalition crisis, 110–11
    friendship with, 18–19, 85, 115
    as leadership candidate, 51–52, 79, 85–86, 91, 108
Rae, Jennifer, 22
Rae, John, 86
Rae, Saul, 18–19
recession
    in Canada, 106–7, 112, 117, 119, 138, 139
    government's role, 139–40
    Harper and, 107, 108, 119, 138
    Liberal Party and, 107, 138–40
Reflections on the Revolution in France (Burke), 169
Renan, Ernest, 39
resilience, 23
Rhodes Scholarships, 10–11, 12, 85
"The Rights Revolution" (Ignatieff), 27
Robertson, Norman, 16
Romney, Mitt, 127
Roosevelt, Franklin, 171
Rose, Jeff, 19
Royal Canadian Mounted Police, 44
Russia, 180

Sakamoto, Mark, 41
science and technology, 74
Second World War, 11–12, 13–15
separatism, 22, 62
Sikand, Baljit, 42, 162
Sikh community, 42, 77
Smith, David, 28, 52
social safety net, 73, 103–4, 140
Special Operations Executive
    (SOE), 13–14
"sponsorship scandal," 44
sports, 174–75
sprezzatura, 57–58
Springsteen, Bruce, 155
St. Laurent, Louis, 60
standing, 126–33
    definition, 126
    and democracy, 133–34
    earning, 127, 129
    loss of, 78, 126, 133
    recovering, 167
    voters and, 127, 130–31, 133
Stein, Janice Gross, 165–66
Stó:l nation (BC), 145
Stornoway, 115–16, 165
swift-boating, 121–22. See also
    attack ads

thought vs. action, 170–71
Tocqueville, Alexis de, 170

Tolstoy, Leo, 174
Toronto, 92–93
torture, 35, 37, 79
Tout le monde en parle (television
    show), 75–76
town hall meetings, 141–42
transportation, 73–74
Trudeau, Pierre, 19–21, 22–24,
    60, 96
trust (earning), 56–57, 59–60,
    131–32, 178
truth
    in attack ads, 122, 123
    vs. loyalty, 148–49
    in politics, 8, 61–62

Ukraine, 36
Ukrainian Canadians, 35–38, 41,
    44–45
unemployment, 139, 140
United Nations, 12
United States of America
    attack ads in, 121–22
    elections in, 70, 71–72, 130, 132–33
    politics in, 16–17, 25, 37
    Supreme Court, 71–72
University of Ottawa, 52
University of Toronto, 18–19, 23,
    165–66, 168–69

Vargas Llosa, Mario, 2

Vietnam War, 19, 21, 121, 122

voters, 42–43, 138
  and attack ads, 129, 132
  earning trust of, 131–32, 178
  political choices, 128, 129, 130, 131, 179–80
  responsibility to, 148, 180
  and standing, 127, 130–31, 133
  views of Parliament, 100, 101, 102–3, 145, 150

war, 174, 181. *See also* Second World War

War and Peace (Tolstoy), 174

Weber, Max, 148, 170, 182

Wright, Jeremiah, 122

Wrong, Hume, 16

Yale (BC), 125–26

Zsohar, Zsuzsanna, 115, 173
  and challenges of politics, 37, 141
  and leadership campaigns, 53, 59, 86–87
  support for Liberal Party, 44, 166
  support for MI, 2, 9, 31, 47